Creating a Culture of Excellence

BRIDGING THEORY AND PRACTICE

Jeffrey Glanz

The motto of this series is framed after Kurt Lewin's famous statement, and I paraphrase, that there is no sound theory without practice and no good practice that is not framed on some theory. The R&L Series is premised on the need to connect theory to practice. We encourage potential contributors to raise important and critical questions that rely on a sound theoretical research base but also find relevance in the world of practice. I welcome readers to join the effort to increase knowledge in our field and affect daily school practice by submitting a book proposal. Feel free to communicate with me via email at yosglanz@gmail.com.

* * * * * * * * * *

Books already published in the series:

Brown, K., & Shaked, H. (2018). *Preparing future leaders for social justice: Bridging theory and practice through a transformative andragogy* (2nd edition). Rowman & Littlefield.

Glanz, J. (Ed.). (2021). *Crisis and pandemic leadership: Implications for meeting the needs of students, teachers, and parents.* Rowman & Littlefield.

Glanz, J. (Ed.). (2021). *Managing today's schools: New skills for school leaders in the 21st century.* Rowman & Littlefield.

Lavigne, A. L., & Derrington, M. L. (Eds.). (2023). *Actionable feedback for PK–12 teachers.* Rowman & Littlefield.

Locke, L. A., & Hayes, S. D. (2024). *Bridging leadership and school improvement: Advice from the field.* Rowman & Littlefield.

Rabinowitz, C., & Reichel, M. (2023). *Principal recruitment and retention: Best practices for meeting the challenges of today.* Rowman & Littlefield.

Shaked, H. (2022). *New explorations for instructional leaders: How principals can promote teaching and learning effectively.* Rowman & Littlefield.

Snyder, K. J., & Snyder, K. M. (Eds.). (2023). *Systems thinking for sustainable schooling: A mindshift for educators to lead and achieve quality schools.* Rowman & Littlefield.

Snyder, K. M., & Snyder, K. J. (Eds.). (2024). *Regenerating education as a living system: Success stories of systems thinking in action.* Rowman & Littlefield.

Stader, D. (2012). *Leadership for a culture of school safety: Linking theory to practice.* Rowman & Littlefield.

Zepeda, S. J. (Ed.). (2018). *Making learning job-embedded: Cases from the field of educational leadership.* Rowman & Littlefield.

Zepeda, S. J. (Ed.). (2018). *The job-embedded nature of coaching: Lessons and insights for school leaders.* Rowman & Littlefield.

Zepeda, S. J. (Ed.). (2008). *Real world supervision: Adapting theory to practice.* Rowman & Littlefield.

Creating a Culture of Excellence

A School Leader's Guide to Best Practices in Teaching, Curriculum, Professional Development, Supervision, and Evaluation

Jeffrey Glanz

ROWMAN & LITTLEFIELD
Lanham • Boulder • New York • London

Published by Rowman & Littlefield
An imprint of The Rowman & Littlefield Publishing Group, Inc.
4501 Forbes Boulevard, Suite 200, Lanham, Maryland 20706
www.rowman.com

86-90 Paul Street, London EC2A 4NE, United Kingdom

Copyright © 2024 by Jeffrey Glanz

All rights reserved. No part of this book may be reproduced in any form or by any electronic or mechanical means, including information storage and retrieval systems, without written permission from the publisher, except by a reviewer who may quote passages in a review.

British Library Cataloguing in Publication Information Available

Library of Congress Cataloging-in-Publication Data

Names: Glanz, Jeffrey author.
Title: Creating a culture of excellence : a school leader's guide to best practices in teaching, curriculum, professional development, supervision, and evaluation / Jeffrey Glanz.
Description: Lanham, MD : Rowman & Littlefield, [2024] | Series: Bridging theory and practice | Includes bibliographical references and index. | Summary: "Creating a Culture of Excellence is a resource that serves as a guide to the best practices in teaching, curriculum, professional development (PD), supervision, and evaluation"— Provided by publisher.
Identifiers: LCCN 2023056433 (print) | LCCN 2023056434 (ebook) | ISBN 9781475874532 (cloth) | ISBN 9781475874549 (paperback) | ISBN 9781475874556 (epub)
Subjects: LCSH: Educational leadership—United States. | School management and organization—United States.
Classification: LCC LB2805 .G524 2024 (print) | LCC LB2805 (ebook) | DDC 371.2/0110973--dc23/eng/20240110
LC record available at https://lccn.loc.gov/2023056433
LC ebook record available at https://lccn.loc.gov/2023056434

Contents

Introduction	vii
Chapter 1: The State of Instructional Quality in Schools	1
Chapter 2: The Key Component of Instructional Quality: The Instructional Core	23
Chapter 3: An Overview of Best Practices in Teaching, Curriculum, Professional Development, Supervision, and Evaluation	45
Chapter 4: Learning to Lead Instructional Change by Transforming School Culture to Support and Improve Teaching and Learning for All	77
Appendix A: State of Teaching, Curriculum, Professional Development, Supervision, and Evaluation (Shortest Version) Questionnaire	93
Appendix B: State of Teaching, Curriculum, Professional Development, Supervision, and Evaluation (Short Version) Questionnaire	97
Appendix C: State of Teaching, Curriculum, Professional Development, Supervision, and Evaluation (Long Version) Questionnaire	103
Appendix D: On-the-Spot Beliefs about Instructional Quality Questionnaire	113
Appendix E: Assessing Your Role as an Instructional Leader and Supervisor Questionnaire	117
Appendix F: Teacher Self-Assessment Questionnaire	125

Appendix G: Supervisor's Perceptions about Teacher's Views
Questionnaire   131

Appendix H: Teacher Attitude Questionnaire   135

Appendix I: Best Annotated Works and Resources for Promoting
Instructional Excellence   139

Appendix J: Sample Instructional Audit Report   155

Appendix K: The Instructional Goals Matrix   165

Index   167

About the Author   169

Call for Submissions: The Rowman & Littlefield Leadership Series:
Bridging Theory and Practice   171
Edited by Jeffrey Glanz, Michlalah-Jerusalem College, Israel

Introduction

Over the past several decades I have been privileged to visit many schools—preschools to high schools—and examine their instructional programs. I have met the people who lead public and private schools who personify the best in the profession. These educators possess an unyielding commitment and inspirational dedication to inculcating sound moral values and knowledge so that all children can succeed academically and socially.

I have also been privileged to serve as a classroom teacher for fifteen years (grades four through eight) and as an assistant principal for five years in an inner-city elementary school (student population 1,500), only then leaving to enter the world of academia as a professor of educational leadership. Over the past thirty years, I have been honored to become conversant with research literature on effective schooling, with particular emphasis on instructional quality. *Creating a Culture of Excellence* is aimed at bringing together personal experiences, experiences and views of practitioners with whom I have been privileged to work, views of international educators, and drawing upon best practices advocated in the research literature to greatly benefit schools to reach even higher levels of instructional and academic excellence.

Although school leaders are dedicated, they confront many daily challenges. These leaders must deal with managerial, political, financial, operational, and communal issues (Craig, 2020), not to mention crises that often arise (Shenhav, 2022). They know, though, that a significant portion of their time must be devoted to promoting educational quality; more specifically, a program of instructional excellence that promotes learning for all students (Hallinger et al., 2020). School leaders are busy, and overwhelmed, and may not always be cognizant of the latest cutting-edge theories and practices in the field of instructional leadership (Grint, 2010). On more than one occasion I have been asked by school leaders for a resource that may serve as a guide to best practices in instructional improvement. This book seeks, in part, to address that need.

This book is unique because it offers an approach to instruction (i.e., instructional quality or improvement) not commonly found in the literature. Often, the term "instruction" is used in the literature and practice as synonymous with "teaching" (Blikstad-Balas et al., 2022). The instructional process most definitely includes teaching. However, without the inclusion of four other elements one cannot understand nor analyze instructional quality in a school (Asian Development Bank, 2011). *Creating a Culture of Excellence* views instruction as a five-fold interrelated process that includes teaching, curriculum, professional development (PD), supervision, and evaluation. In other words, assessing a school's instructional program involves investigating each of these five elements in consonance with one another (Glanz, 1997).

Two contrasting conceptions or approaches to education, at large, may help to understand the instructional process, in particular (Kestel & Korkmaz, 2019). From a modernistic perspective, education is conceived as a static process of transmitting knowledge, skills, and values of society. Teaching, in this light, becomes necessary to impart this knowledge, cultural expectations, and ethical ideals. The teaching-learning process is viewed as a "banking concept," as articulated by Paulo Freire (1974). In other words, teachers talk, and students listen. Learning is a process of accepting ready-made bits of information that the student must recall on examinations. Supervision, in this context, becomes an inspectional process to ensure compliance with mandated curricula and evaluative requirements.

In contrast, a postmodern perspective views education as an ongoing, spirited engagement that a learner undertakes (Starratt, 1993; Tesar et al., 2021). Education is best conceived from its etymological Latin context meaning "to draw out or to lead." The goal of a teacher is to draw out that latent potential within every student (Schutz, 2000). Representative of such a view, for example, is the work of Nel Noddings (2005) who made the point, "We should educate all our children not only for competence but also for caring. Our aim should be to encourage the growth of competent, caring, loving, and lovable people" (p. xiv).

Instruction, the core process that can actualize society's goals via the process of schooling, be it based on a modernistic or postmodern perspective, accomplishes its stated aims via a mechanism we call curriculum. Instruction and curriculum are inextricably connected. Instruction is the process that translates, if you will, the curriculum into practice. It involves an understanding of the process in which people learn, it includes teaching practices to ensure that learning occurs and that curricular goals are achieved, and it involves other ideas that support teaching and learning (Goldhawk, 2023). These may include, among others, administrative policies, ethical and legal imperatives, and more closely connected to teaching and learning, the supervision of instruction (Glanz & Behar-Horenstein, 2000).

A review of the literature over the past fifty years or so indicates that instruction, erroneously, became associated or synonymous with the teaching act itself (Hoetker & Ahlbrand, 1969). The emergence of a new concept known as *instructional leadership* helped clarify previous misconceptions and broaden knowledge about how best to promote student learning. Instructional leadership entails a variety of leadership initiatives aimed at promoting student learning and achievement. Therefore, instructional leaders, among other initiatives, may help facilitate curriculum development, establish a conducive organizational culture or climate to support instruction, create a meaningful teacher evaluation program, create a professional learning community to unify individuals involved in promoting instructional excellence, and set up a supervisory process that encourages teachers to reflect upon and improve their teaching. In other words, instructional leadership involves supporting the school, instructionally, on macroscopic and microscopic levels (Shaked, 2022). In contrast, supervision is more focused on supporting teachers in the classroom (Coppola, 2004; Ducker & Holmberg, 2023; Miller, 2023) and teacher evaluation moves beyond its historic accountability function to support student learning (Hazi & Rucinski, 2009).

Therefore, this book is unique because it examines instructional quality holistically by addressing its major components, or five critical dimensions (teaching, curriculum, PD, supervision, and evaluation), in an integrated fashion. *Creating a Culture of Excellence* summarizes extant research and literature in the field of instructional leadership by providing practical recommendations to enhance a school's instructional program. The book includes four main chapters:

- Chapter 1 extrapolates the state of instructional quality from extant data drawn from research literature as well as from reports from the field (e.g., Darling-Hammond, 2000; Heck, 2007; Senden et al., 2022). A questionnaire (one of three versions found in appendices A, B, and C) was sent to educators in several countries to ascertain perceptions of instructional quality in their schools. The questionnaire (Appendix A) focuses on the nature of five key instructional dimensions: teaching, curriculum, PD, supervision, and evaluation (all essential components of any instructional program). The ideas in this chapter (and book) are also based on personal observations and experiences (Glanz, 2012). The findings are tentative and not generalizable to all schools. Yet the survey does give a glimpse into the nature of instruction. Readers are encouraged to reflect on the findings based on their own school experiences.

    Findings indicate that schools have much in common (for the positive and, unfortunately, the not-so-positive, for example, the persistence of recitation is all too common at all levels of schooling, outdated curricula

or overuse of packed curricula, mandated PD that is seen as irrelevant and boring to teachers, an onerous evaluation system, inspectional supervisory practices, and bureaucratic mandates from ministries or departments of education).
- Chapter 2 presents a theoretical framework for understanding the components of instructional quality. It focuses on a concept known as "the instructional core," which guides the manner in which school leaders might improve instruction (City et al., 2009). Extant research indicates that reliance on the instructional core will positively impact teaching (Tekkumnu-Kisa et al., 2022), PD (Mchenry et al., 2017), and supervision (Glickman et al., 2017). Curriculum development should be premised on the Instructional Core (Rivet Education, 2021) as should teacher evaluation (City, 2011). School leaders who rely on this core will be in a better position to improve their school's instructional program.
- Chapter 3 is the most practical chapter in that research-based techniques and strategies for teaching, curriculum, PD, supervision, and evaluation as best practices, are presented. Readers are encouraged to reflect on their practicality and ease of implementation.
- Chapter 4, the final chapter, encourages school leaders to reflect on their school's instructional program, undertake strategic planning, and make appropriate and relevant changes for improvement. The process for change is discussed by drawing from the literature on school change. A case study is then presented to highlight the manner in which one high school principal was committed to improving their school's instructional program. In analyzing the case, challenges encountered and opportunities for improvement are discussed. The case study provides an approach to instructional change with the hope that other school leaders can follow suit.

Eleven appendices (A–K) conclude the book. The information contained in them is important for five reasons:

1. Appendices A, B, and C represent three versions of varying lengths of the same questionnaire to assess the five basic aspects of a school's instructional program: teaching, curriculum, PD, supervision, and evaluation. Readers may want to use these questionnaires to gather information in different contexts for varying purposes.
2. They provide five self-assessment reflective tools in the form of questionnaires to assess school leaders' beliefs, attitudes, and practices related to instructional leadership and, in particular, to their instructional program (Appendices D, E, F, G, and H).

Introduction xi

3. Appendix I, in particular, provides an invaluable and comprehensive annotated list of works and resources for promoting instructional excellence.
4. Appendix J, discussed in Chapter 1, provides a report based on an actual school instructional assessment that gives readers an example of a comprehensive survey of a school's instructional programming.
5. Finally, Appendix K discussed in Chapter 2 provides readers with a tool to guide setting goals in a strategic way for establishing and assessing an instructional program.

Each chapter includes a synopsis of ideas to be covered as well as Guiding Questions to stimulate and encourage thinking of key ideas and concepts discussed in the chapter. Interspersed are vignettes that are drawn from actual classrooms and other school contexts. Thought-provoking activities will help review content and encourage readers to consider the manner in which various best practices might be implemented in their schools.

* * *

This book is part of the Rowman & Littlefield (R&L) School Leadership Series: Bridging Theory and Practice whose motto is framed after Kurt Lewin's famous statement, and I paraphrase, that there is no sound theory without practice and no good practice that is not framed on some theory. The R&L series is premised on the need to connect theory to practice. Potential contributors are encouraged to raise critical questions that have a sound theoretical research base but also find relevance to the world of practice. The series and this book are supported by Thomas Koerner, PhD (former vice president and senior executive editor, who retired in 2023). I would like to thank him for his support in publishing *Creating a Culture of Excellence*. Special thanks to Jasmine Holman, assistant editor. Thanks also to David Bailey, production editor, for diligent efforts in producing the manuscript in its final stages.

Thanks are also extended to the many school leaders who offered their insights and suggestions. My career has been spent attempting to help educators draw from well-researched best practices to establish meaningful and effective pedagogies and instructional strategies to help children grow and learn. I would appreciate hearing from readers about their reactions to the ideas offered in this volume as well as their comments, questions, and suggestions. I can be contacted at yosglanz@gmail.com.

REFERENCES

Asian Development Bank. (2011, December). *Improving instructional quality: Focus on faculty development*. Asian Development Bank. https://www.adb.org/sites/default/files/publication/29437/improving-instructional-quality.pdf

Blikstad-Balas, M., Klette, K., & Tengberg, M. (Eds.). (2022). *Ways of analyzing teaching quality: Potentials and pitfalls*. Unversiteforlaget. https://doi.org/10.18261/9788215045054-2021

City, E. A. (2011). Learning from instructional rounds. https://www.ascd.org/el/articles/learning-from-instructional-rounds

City, E. A., Elmore, R. F., Fiarman, S. E., & Teitel, L. (2009). *Instructional rounds in education: A network approach to improving teaching and learning*. Harvard Educational Press.

Coppola, A. J., Scricca, D. B., & Connors, G. E. (2004). *Supportive supervision: Becoming a teacher of teachers*. Corwin.

Craig, I. (2020). Whatever happened to educational management? The case for reinstatement. *Management in Education, 35*(1), 52–57. https://doi.org/10.1177/0892020620962813

Darling-Hammond, L. (2000). *Teacher quality and student achievement: A review of state policy evidence*. Center for the Study of Teaching and Policy, University of Washington.

Ducker, B., & Holmberg, C. (2023). *Feedback for continuous improvement in the classroom: New perspectives, practices, and possibilities*. Sage.

Freire, P. (1974). *Pedagogy of the oppressed*. The Free Press.

Glanz, J. (1997). Interrelationships among curriculum, instruction, teaching, learning, administration, and supervision: A postmodernist interpretation. *National Forum of Educational Administration and Supervision Journal, 10*(1), 18–23.

Glanz, J., & Behar-Horenstein, L. (2000). *Paradigm debates in curriculum and supervision: Modern and postmodern perspectives*. Bergin & Garvey.

Glanz, J. (2012). *Improving instructional quality in Jewish day schools: Best practices culled from research and practices in the field*. The Azrieli Papers, Yeshiva University.

Glickman, C. D., Gordon, S. P., & Ross-Gordon, J. M. (2017). *SuperVision and instructional leadership: A developmental approach* (10th ed.). Pearson.

Goldhawk, A. (2023). *The super quick guide to learning theories and teaching approaches*. Sage.

Grint, K. (2010). Wicked problems and clumsy solutions: The role of leadership. In S. Brookes & K. Grint (Eds.), *The new public leadership challenge*. Palgrave Macmillan, London. https://doi.org/10.1057/9780230277953_11

Hallinger, P., Gumus, S., & Bellibas, M. S. (2020). Are principals instructional leaders yet? A science map of the knowledge base on instructional leadership. *Scientometrics, 122*(3), 1629–1650. doi.org/10.1007/s11192-020-03360-5Scopus Q1

Hazi, H., & Rucinski, D. A. (2009). Teacher evaluation as a policy target for improved student learning: A fifty-state review of the statute and regulatory action since

NCLB. *Education Policy Analysis Archives, 17*(5). https://doi.org/10.14507/epaa.v17n5.2009

Heck, R. H. (2007). Examining the relationship between teacher quality as an organizational property of schools and students' achievement and growth rates. *Educational Administration Quarterly, 43*(4), 399–432.

Hoetker, J., & Ahlbrand, W. P., Jr. (1969). The persistence of the recitation. *American Education Research Journal, 6*, 145–167. https://doi.org/10.3102/00028312006002145

Kestel, M., & Korkmaz, I. (2019). The impact of modernism and postmodernism on teaching. *Turquoise International Journal of Educational Research and Social Studies, 1*(1), 28–33. https://eric.ed.gov/?id=ED596101

Mchenry, N., Borgor, L., & Liable-Sands, L. (2017). A novel approach to professional development in middle school science: Instructional coaching by university professors to improve the instructional core. *Journal of Curriculum and Teaching 6*(2), 59–74. https://eric.ed.gov/?id=EJ1157425

Miller, L. S. (2023). Supervision to support reflective practices. *Journal of Educational Supervision, 6*(1). https://doi.org/10.31045/jes.6.1.1

Noddings, N. (2005). *The challenge to care in schools: An alternative approach to education* (2nd ed.). Teachers College Press.

Rivet Education. (2021). The call for expanding the instructional core. https://riveteducation.org/the-call-for-expanding-the-instructional-core-engaging-families-in-curriculum-implementation-to-maximize-student-learning/

Schutz, A. (2000). Teaching freedom? Postmodernism perspectives. *Review of Educational Research, 70*(2), 215–251. https://doi.org/10.3102/00346543070002215

Senden, R., Nilsen, T., & Blomeke, S. (2022). Instructional quality: A review of conceptualizations, measurement approaches, and research findings. In M. Blikstad-Balas, K. Klette, & M. Tengberg (Eds.), *Ways of analyzing teaching quality: Potentials and pitfalls* (pp. 14–172). Unversiteforlaget. https://doi.org/10.18261/9788215045054-2021-05

Shaked, H. (2022). *New explorations for instructional leaders: How principals can promote teaching and learning effectively.* Rowman & Littlefield.

Shenhav, S. (2022). Pedagogical leadership during crisis: The shift to distance learning in an Israeli religious college during COVID-19. *Journal of Practitioner Research, 7*(1). https://digitalcommons.usf.edu/jpr/vol7/iss1/5

Starratt, R. J. (1993). *The drama of leadership.* Routledge.

Tekkumnu-Kisa, M., Akcil-Okan, O., Kisa, Z., & Sotherland, S. (2022). Exploring science teaching in teaching as the instructional core. *Journal of Research in Science Teaching, 60*(1), 26–62. https://onlinelibrary.wiley.com/doi/epdf/10.1002/tea.21790

Tesar, M., Gibbons, A., Arndt, S., & Hood, N. (2021). Postmodernism in education. *Oxford Research Encyclopedias.* https://doi.org/10.1093/acrefore/9780190264093.013.1269

Chapter 1

The State of Instructional Quality in Schools

This chapter aims to bring understanding and reflection upon the nature and practice of teaching, curriculum, professional development (PD), supervision, and evaluation in selected schools internationally. The chapter is based on personal observations as well as the results of a study surveying instructional practices in schools in several countries. These schools have much in common (dedicated educators who work arduously despite low remuneration, lack of sufficient recognition, and challenging circumstances; and, unfortunately, the persistence of recitation that is all too common at all levels of schooling, outdated curricula, or the over-reliance on packed curricula, mandated PD that is seen as irrelevant and boring to teachers, an onerous evaluation system, inspectional supervisory practices, and persistence of bureaucratic mandates from ministries or departments of education). The chapter will report on the status of instruction at large with examples culled from the field as reported by various observers and participants. The findings are tentative to the extent that no one can generalize based on a relatively small sample and to all facets of schooling. We leave it up to the reader to determine the validity of the findings as well as consider the best practices discussed later in the book.

FOCUS QUESTIONS

1. Given your personal experiences in the field, how would you characterize the nature of teaching in schools?
2. Can you list some of the best and worst teaching practices you have witnessed?
3. What constraints might teachers encounter that prevent them from teaching optimally?

4. Using the questions above as a guide, comment on the nature of curriculum development, PD, supervision, and teacher evaluation.
5. Why should there be an alignment among teaching, curriculum, PD, supervision, and teacher evaluation? What would an ideal alignment look like in practice?

Curriculum, instruction, assessment, professional development, supervision, and evaluation are not independent or isolated activities. They are interconnected and interdependent. They are part of a complex, dynamic system that must be understood as a whole if we are to improve student learning.

—Thomas Sergiovanni, 2005

INTRODUCTION: THE EMERGENCE OF INSTRUCTIONAL LEADERSHIP

Instructional leadership is one of the most significant responsibilities of a school leader. Many researchers have shown the importance of high-quality instruction as a necessary component of student improvement and achievement (Cruickshank, 2017; Hitt, 2011; Tedla & Kilango, 2022). Yet despite this fairly recent awareness of the importance of the principal's role as an instructional leader, attention to it is limited (Brazer & Bauer, 2013; Flessa, 2012). Even in many countries it is still not viewed as a primary responsibility of a principal (Hallinger & Lee, 2013; Loveless, 2016; OECD, 2022). Principals as managers rather than instructional leaders dominate discourse in many quarters. Moreover, even when leaders realize its necessity, many inhibiting factors prevent these leaders from spending significant time in addressing instructional matters (Shaked, 2018). Without a serious and ongoing commitment to instructional improvement, instructional matters are too often taken for granted or slip through the proverbial crack (Goldring et al., 2015; Shaked, 2021a).

According to Shaked (2021b), instructional leadership is an educational leadership model in which principals are directly and continually involved in curricular and instructional issues. His study attempts to provide a basis for instructional leadership work in four areas: (1) with leaders themselves, (2) with school middle leaders, (3) with teachers, and (4) with external stakeholders. Shaked's work is representative of current research and literature that indicates that *instructional leadership* is part of the larger theoretical frame known as *educational leadership*.

In other words, educational leadership, as demonstrated by a review of the literature in extant books and journals, encompasses many more broad areas including, among others, leaders who work in varied contexts, not just schools, and leaders who lead in multifaceted ways including managing the organization, fundraising initiatives, and financial and legal matters. Instructional leadership, then, is viewed as one particular arena in which educational leaders may operate, that is, in the realm of matters related to the instructional process.

Instructional leadership emerged from the literature on transformational leadership. Transformational leadership emerged from the literature on school change in an attempt to more broadly reform and improve schools. It relied on the literature of "change knowledge," partly promulgated through Michael Fullan's (2008) work in his discussion of the "key drivers for change" specifically related to attending to and transforming a school's culture. Transformational school leadership theory provided support for such efforts.

* * *

Transformational leadership, according to Northouse (2003), was "first coined by Downton" (1973 as cited by Northouse, 2003, p. 131). Yet it is acknowledged widely that James MacGregor Burns amplified this approach to leadership in a landmark book titled *Leadership* in 1978. Burns, according to Northouse (2003), identified two types of leadership: transactional (managerial) and transformational (visionary). The former represented the everyday interactions between manager and follower. Offering an incentive, for instance, to a follower for procedural compliance to school policy reflects transactional leadership. In contrast, transformational leadership engaged people around an ethical and moral vision of excellence for all.

Another version of transformational leadership emerged with the work of House (1976), interestingly around the same time that Burns published his work. House's leadership construct focused on a leader's charisma. Charismatic, transformational leaders possess personal characteristics that include "being dominant, having a strong desire to influence others, being self-confident, and having a strong sense of one's own moral values" (p. 132).

Later, a version of transformational leadership emerged in the work of Bass (1985). Bass extended House's work by placing greater attention on the needs of followers rather than the leader and that charisma by itself did not encapsulate all there is to know about transformational leadership. His model also more explicitly addressed how transformational leaders go about their work. According to Northouse (2003), "Transformational leadership helps followers to transcend their own self-interests for the good of the group or organization" (p. 137). Transformational leadership did not provide a recipe for leading but rather a way of thinking that emphasized visionary and participatory leadership.

* * *

Transformational leadership received much attention in the educational leadership literature (see, e.g., Leithwood & Jantzi, 2005). Although transformational leadership had been examined by other theorists (House, 1976), Leithwood and Jantzi (2005) addressed the implications of transformational leadership for schools. According to them, "three broad categories of leadership practices" could be identified: setting directions, developing people, and redesigning the organization. The authors explained that setting directions is a "critical aspect of transformational leadership . . . [by] . . . helping staff to develop shared understandings about the school and its activities as well as the goals that undergird a sense of purpose or vision" (pp. 38–39). They explained that people are more likely to participate when they have a say in developing ideas and practices. Transformational leaders realize that anyone can set a direction for an organization, but it is the effective leader who considers and solicits the participation of other key school personnel to share in the development and actualization of the institutional vision and purpose.

It was based on these latter two categories that greater emphasis was placed on transforming a school's instructional program. Those who advocated transformational leadership realized that although change was needed at the organizational level of a school, equally essential was attention to the "inner core" of a school, that is, the school's instructional program whose purpose was to raise student achievement.

This work on transformational leadership led, more so than ever before, to a reexamination of a school's commitment to teacher quality, teacher growth, instructional excellence, and student learning. Although the ensuing work in the field addressed several different areas, attention to what become known as the "Instructional Core" became the lynchpin of the literature on instructional leadership. In other words, transformational leaders were to work in an effort to alter school culture by nurturing a professional learning community (Sullivan & Glanz, 2006) in which leaders would serve as change agents or facilitators of change to actualize their vision for instructional excellence (Fullan, 2006). Instructional quality became the main focus to transform teaching and learning (Shava & Heystek, 2021).

Consequently, the focus on instructional improvement (quality) became marked. Developing and managing the organizational structures that facilitate and support the school's instructional programming became critical. Instructional leaders primarily aimed to transform teaching and learning in alignment with the school's mission, evaluate instruction and programs, and facilitate curriculum and professional development by creating professional learning communities to promote student learning and achievement.

THE STATE OF INSTRUCTIONAL QUALITY IN SELECTED SCHOOLS IN TERMS OF TEACHING PRACTICES, CURRICULUM DEVELOPMENT, PROFESSIONAL DEVELOPMENT, SUPERVISION, AND EVALUATION

Creating a Culture of Excellence initially emerged from the work of a team of educational specialists that visited, over a two-day period, 39 schools throughout North America over a three-year period wherein "instructional audits" were conducted at the behest of school boards, local school administrators, local school districts, and sometimes ministries or departments of education. These instructional audits varied in depth and comprehensiveness. During a typical visit, the team observed many class sessions at all relevant grade levels, interviewed teachers, parents, selected students, school officials, learning specialists, district administrators, union officials, and board members. Relevant instructionally related documents were collected and analyzed.

A school operates as a system (Snyder & Snyder, 2023) that entails many fundamental and interrelated aspects including, for instance, its culture, staffing, leadership structure, partnerships, financial state, etc. The visits described above, in brief, examined the five instructional dimensions considering the larger context in which they functioned. However, this book focuses more narrowly on the five dimensions (teaching, curriculum, PD, supervision, and evaluation) in and of themselves, as they are the most critical aspects of a school's instructional program, as explained in the introduction. Other books take a broader, less focused view (Shaked et al., 2018).

Exhibit A outlines the preparatory phase for an "instructional audit." Schools, in preparation for such a visit, are asked to attend to the items in it.

In Appendix J, readers will find replicated, without identifying information, a sample instructional audit report that this author wrote that was shared with the school after a two-day visit to assess instructional quality. In many cases, schools wanted a follow-up meeting(s) to assist them in implementing some of the suggestions made in the report.

During 2022 to 2023, responses to a questionnaire (see Appendix A) that was distributed via Google Forms to colleagues in several countries were received.[1] This chapter highlights findings from that questionnaire as well as reports from the field as indicated above regarding the instructional audits that were conducted.

EXHIBIT A

ARTIFACTS TO COLLECT BEFORE SITE VISIT AND DOMAINS FOR EXAMINATION

Prior to our visit to your school, please provide us with as many of the following pieces of information as is readily available. The list of documents or artifacts is merely suggestive. Please feel free to include any data you deem relevant for the team to obtain as clear a picture of your instructional programming as possible.

School demographics: E.g., relevant historical information, #s of administrators, teachers, support staff, students, etc.

Teacher demographics: E.g., degrees, licenses, educational background, years of experience, tenure status, etc.

Administrator demographics: E.g., degrees, licenses, educational background, years of experience, etc.

School data that inform instructional, programming: E.g., school climate survey data (solicited from teachers, students, &/or parents); satisfaction data, class composition and class size data, tracked classes/subjects, acceptance rates (high schools, colleges), teacher/student/parent handbooks, policy manuals, etc.

Administration: E.g., vision statements related to instructional programming, bulletins/memos related to instructional programming, schedule of teacher/faculty meetings (agenda, etc.), meeting minutes, or summaries, etc.

Curriculum: E.g., handbooks, sequence charts, maps, lesson plan samples for grades/subjects, etc.

Assessment: E.g., formative and summative assessment summaries, student score summaries on standardized tests (past two years), teacher or administrator-created summative assessments for grades, etc.

PD: E.g., formalized plans for PD, planned schedule of activities for prior three years (including # of days, topics, etc.), list of out-of-school PD opportunities, PD budget line specifics, etc.

Supervision: E.g., schedules of teacher observations, sample write-ups, if any, professional growth plans, etc.

Evaluation: E.g., documents that explain the process utilized, sample copies of evaluations (with names blocked out), explanations of how evaluations are used, schedules, etc.

Teaching: E.g., grade conference meetings/topics, steps taken to improve teaching, innovative teaching practices, particular philosophies adopted by the school, etc.

Domains of School Functioning to be Examined During the Visit:

Guiding Principles and Core Beliefs

- Examine the school mission statement, or statement of vision, and how that vision is infused into all areas of the school. Identify the extent of consensus around the vision. If warranted, assist the school to articulate a useful vision statement that is comprehensible and meaningful to parents, board, and faculty.

Academics

- Assess graduation requirements and the extent to which they meet and/or exceed minimum state requirements and field-wide standards;
- Assess each department's goals, objectives, and course offerings;
- Examine school practices and beliefs regarding student assessment, grading, ability-level grouping, etc.; and
- Observe instruction to note general areas of strength and weakness.

Student Life

- Identify school practices and beliefs regarding co-curricular activities, leadership opportunities for students, etc.; and
- Assess processes and policies for discipline, attendance, and other school rules based on field practices and the school's vision.

Student Services

- Examine the ways in which academic support is provided for students, including study skills, time management, modified programs, enrichment options, special education services; mainstreaming (inclusion), etc.; and
- Assess the school's capacity to provide guidance and counseling support for students to ensure their healthy emotional development.

School Climate for Students and Faculty

- Formally or informally assess the impact of all of the above on school climate as experienced by students and teachers.

Leadership Structure

- Identify understaffed areas of school administration if they exist;
- Identify potential professional development and growth opportunities for administration professionals and faculty; and
- Assess board composition and functioning, identifying areas that could be strengthened.

Fiscal Sustainability

- Assess the strength of the school's fiscal status;
- Examine school processes related to budget and financial management to identify areas that could be strengthened;
- Identify specific strategic challenges faced by the school, such as acquiring new facilities.

Results indicate that many schools face seemingly intractable educational challenges. Yet once again, it should be emphasized that these and other schools have also excelled in many ways, including

- dedicated faculty who work hard to help children grow academically, emotionally, and socially;
- committed school leaders (principals, their assistants, and other supervisors, whether situated in the school, district, or ministry) who believe that their work is sacred to help children succeed in every possible way;
- supportive board members, district leaders, and other lay personnel who deeply believe in the school's mission and go out of their way to support the school to accomplish its lofty mission of educating every child; and
- competent specialists and support staff who care deeply about their work.

Creating a Culture of Excellence aims to identify key instructional challenges with the expectation that educational leaders will consider implementing the recommendations offered. Instructional improvement through transformational school-wide change is discussed and encouraged.

TEACHING

I want to begin by mentioning a word about teaching since without an understanding of its dimensions, discussion of curriculum and the other instructional processes is limited. If someone mentions the word "instruction," then teaching immediately comes to mind. In fact, instruction is a more encompassing process that includes curriculum, PD, supervision, and evaluation as well. However, if one is to fully understand the instructional process, then a deep understanding of teaching is required. Stop a moment and do this activity:

Learning Activity #1

Define the word "teaching."

_____

_____

Effective teachers can organize their ideas in such a way that is logical, sequential, visual, and complete. They are enthusiastic, caring, articulate, sensitive to student needs, and possess a host of several other desirable characteristics. However, on a technical level, they are conversant with the art and science of teaching. Effective teachers view teaching as an intentional process that encourages students to actively engage (cognitively, affectively, and/or in a psychomotor capacity) with content and that the process ensures that learning occurs through activities known as assessment (i.e., Checking for Understanding, or CFU), and feedback (because if one merely checks without remedying deficiencies, then learning has not likely occurred, and, therefore, "teaching" has similarly not occurred).

Teaching is not merely conveying information (Hoetker & Ahlbrand, 1969); that's known as lecturing, which can indeed be used during the teaching process. However, by itself it is inadequate. Our research indicates that it is overused, and therefore optimal learning is unlikely to occur with most students. Most people don't learn by simply listening because most people are not good auditory learners. They require at least visual stimulation. But that too is insufficient by itself.

Teaching, then, is a twofold intentional process: one, wherein conditions are created in which others interact with content and two, when student comprehension is ensured through an assessment process that includes checking for understanding and feedback (Glanz, 2016). Learning occurs best when teachers actively engage with their students and provide continuous checking for understanding with appropriate feedback when necessary (Hattie & Timperley, 2007).

This understanding is critical because it has implications for the way we construct or develop curricula, the manner in which PD is conceived and offered, as well as the way we supervise and evaluate teachers.

Learning Activity #2

React to the definition of teaching presented above, and discuss the precise implications for implementing curriculum, PD, supervision, and evaluation:

THE STATE ON INSTRUCTION: A SUMMARY OF FINDINGS

This chapter is framed on findings from many school visits, reports from educators in the field, and extant literature in books, journals, and magazines. The example as represented in Table 1.1 is fictional. In reality, it is somewhat representative of certain aspects of different schools and illustrates the difficulties as well as possibilities that exist in many schools. The remainder of the chapter will present more specific information on each of the five instructional areas highlighting several important problematic issues. Later, in Chapter 3, recommendations for improvement in each area are presented.

More on Teaching: Findings and Experiences from the Field

Overuse of Frontal Teaching

Despite small class sizes, frontal teaching (also called direct teaching) is the dominant model utilized in many schools. Some high school educators dubiously defend the practice by explaining that they are preparing students for college. College preparation, they say, requires "us to cover the material, and teaching this way is the best way of meeting that goal." Frontal teaching as a practice is reminiscent of a more accurate description or phrase found in the literature of educational research, that is, "the persistence of recitation" (Hoetker & Ahlbrand, 1969). Research based on scientific observations of classroom discourse, since the early part of the last century, repeatedly demonstrated the persistence of recitation in the classroom (e.g., Biddle & Raymond, 1967).[2]

The three most relevant findings from this research are (1) the great amount of talking done by both good and poor teachers; (2) the short responses made

Table 1.1 Consultant's Report on Instructional Quality

Observations and Suggestions

TEACHING
- Teachers at Stanford Academy (SA) care very much about the educational progress of each student. Despite the noble efforts to incorporate differentiated instruction, many classes exhibit an overuse of frontal teaching (recitation) as the dominant mode of teaching. Although group work and differentiation were evident in lower grades, they were almost absent in the upper grades. Teachers need better preparation on an ongoing basis in differentiated instruction. Some teachers reported comfort in differentiation while many others did not. Also, an overreliance on summative rather than formative assessment was observed. We were particularly impressed with several of the recent hires who appear to be outstanding educators. Although a formal program with adequate PD (read below) for teacher mentoring doesn't exist, new teachers do receive adequate mentoring from their supervisors and in some cases from fellow teachers. Teachers in the school feel supported. Teachers sometimes discuss teaching practices in informal ways. [Evidence: Observations of classrooms form the basis of this conclusion as well as interviews with teachers.]

PROFESSIONAL DEVELOPMENT
- Although SA has provided PD opportunities for teachers, they have been inconsistently employed and not developed strategically, nor with teacher input. These workshops are not assessed in terms of their quality or relevance to teachers' work in the classroom. [Evidence: Interviews and a perusal of documentation were undertaken. PD is acknowledged by school administrators and teachers as needing improvement. Twenty thousand dollars for PD (.004% of the overall budget of $4.5 million) is inadequate, in comparison with similar schools, to accomplish the instructional recommendations outlined in this report.]

CURRICULUM DEVELOPMENT
- Development of curriculum in all subjects needs more ongoing, comprehensive attention, although a start has been made in general studies with the Ontario curricular guidelines. The mere existence of these standards and prepackaged curricula, however, does not imply that curriculum development is ongoing. Curriculum development involves deep, and ongoing conversations collaboratively refined by both administrators and teachers. End-of-year conversations should take place among teachers regarding the effectiveness of the curriculum. Teachers at different grade levels rarely converse over curricula issues. [Evidence: Interviews and interactions with teachers and examination of various curricula.]

SUPERVISION
- Although traditional forms of supervision are practiced (i.e., announced and sometimes unannounced classroom visits), cutting-edge supervisory strategies are not yet utilized. Most teachers shared their ambivalence with this "dog and pony" type observation. One representative teacher stated, "I'd rather them just pop into my room anytime rather than have to put on a meaningless show for them." A greater variety of supervisory approaches are needed, as explained in the body of the report. More formalized use of intervisitations (releasing teachers to observe each other), for instance, is recommended. Additional one-on-one PD within the classrooms to assist teachers to implement differentiated instruction (DI) is recommended. For many teachers, the difference between instructional supervision and teacher evaluation remains unclear. [Evidence: Interviews with administrators and teachers support this finding as well as an examination of related documents.]

Observations and Suggestions

EVALUATION
- Untenured teachers are formally evaluated twice yearly and tenured faculty once a year. The criteria used on the evaluation form have been in existence for the past ten years without revision, until recently. Supervisors have not had formal conversations about the utility of these criteria. A common vision for good teaching in the school is needed and one that is collaboratively developed by administrators and teachers. More recently, however, a form, based on Charlette Danielson's four domains for teacher competency has been adopted by administrators. The form itself merely lists her four categories with a few descriptors and without a precise explanation of the meaning of terms such as "satisfactory," "unsatisfactory," or "stellar performance." Comments made by evaluators are subjective. There is no indication that such evaluations change teaching behavior or improve instruction. It does, however, serve as an accountability function and contractual obligation.

by students; and (3) the large number of questions asked by both good and poor teachers. The nature of questions posed, research indicates, remains at low levels of knowledge and comprehension according to Bloom's (1956) Taxonomy scale. Moreover, recitation is often unidirectional, that is, from teacher to student and back to the teacher. Rarely do students find the need to listen to each other's responses since conversations are controlled and repeated by the teacher.

Teachers, according to further research, address their attention to only one-third of the pupils in a given 40-minute period. The idea or conception of the learning model that has emerged in practice is that for the most part, "teaching is talking, and learning is listening." Based on research on active learning (Breslow, 2020), the educational process most conducive to student learning should be, rather, "learning is talking and teaching is listening (and facilitating learning)" (Hayes & Matusov, 2005).

Frontal teaching appears more advantageous, according to some educators, because their "classes are homogenously grouped, for the most part." Such thinking, although not uncommon, is myopic according to many educators because it assumes that frontal teaching is the preferred approach even for above-average learners.

Frontal teaching, although employed in a differentiated classroom, is minimized. The need for educating teachers in differentiated instruction is axiomatic (Benjamin, 2002, 2003). Educating teachers in differentiated instruction and inclusive practices so that they learn best how to meet the needs of all ability levels within the same classroom is similarly axiomatic (Tomlinson, 2001, 2005).

Vignette #1: When a school administrator was confronted with the fact that all classes in most subjects were tracked and that instruction and curriculum in the lower tracks appeared to be excessively dumbed down and excessively frontal, the response was the following: "Well, you know, some students can't learn as quickly as others and we do take into consideration each child's potential for learning and gear instruction best suited to their learning needs. Besides, it is nearly impossible for a teacher to address all of the learning needs if we heterogeneously mixed our classes."

Some false assumptions:

1. Learning is measured by how "quickly" students absorb the content.
2. Teaching a heterogeneous class is not pedagogically sound nor fair to the "slower" students (or to the "brighter" students for that matter).

Learning Activity #3

What are your feelings about the comment by the school administrator in Vignette 1? How would you respond in a way that would not antagonize him? After all, according to most educators, he appears to have strongly held beliefs, even though they are not educationally sound.

CURRICULUM: FINDINGS AND EXPERIENCES FROM THE FIELD

Lack of Understanding about Curriculum Development

The development of curriculum in general, throughout most subjects, in many schools needs more ongoing, comprehensive attention. An overreliance on prepackaged curricula or top-down curriculum mandates dominant several school systems. Ninety-five percent of survey respondents lamented the top-down, hierarchical policy of boards or ministries of education regarding curriculum development and implementation.

Moreover, many educators have little knowledge of the curriculum development process and what a curriculum is supposed to look like (Tanner & Tanner, 2006). Most curricula are outlined by topics on sheets. No articulation exists in many schools. Curricula are generated by administrators, for the most part, without teacher input. In some cases, teachers themselves develop curricula in isolation of others. Teachers at different grade levels rarely converse over curricular issues (Wiles, 2008).

Vignette #2: When a school administrator was confronted with the observation that formalized curricula in written form were nearly absent in the school, the response was: *"Well, you know, you're right. It is hard to develop a curriculum, but we do hire competent teachers. We do have a list of topics that we require all instructors to follow. We also have worksheets for teachers to use. For most academic subjects we simply use state curriculum standards, so there is little need for curriculum development in these subjects."*

Another administrator in Texas reported, *"Curriculum here is well-mapped and organized, but based on the high stakes achievement test."*

Some false assumptions made by the first administrator are:

1. Curriculum consists of just topics and worksheets.
2. Competent teachers can develop curricula on their own.

Learning Activity #4

What is your reaction to the comment made by the first school administrator?

_____

_____

Learning Activity #5

What is your reaction to the comment made by the second school administrator? What are the advantages and disadvantages of a "well-mapped" curriculum tied to an achievement test? What are your thoughts on state-imposed curricula?

_____

_____

PROFESSIONAL DEVELOPMENT: FINDINGS AND EXPERIENCES FROM THE FIELD

Lack of PD and Common Meeting Time for Faculty

PD is episodic and inconsistent at many schools. Although there are usually monthly faculty meetings, they infrequently deal with instruction. One representative respondent commented, "In most of our faculty meetings, the principal raises administrative and noninstructional related topics."

More specifically, PD is often top-down and initiated without meaningful input by teachers. Teachers often have no input in the topics chosen for the once-yearly workshop, and so at times the teachers tended to perceive the sessions as "a waste of time" or "not relevant to me." No wonder so many teachers find PD useless. Best practices demonstrate that instructional quality is improved by continued in-school learning by all educators (Yendol-Hoppey & Fichtman-Dana, 2010).

PD as a key part of the dimension of managing the instructional program falls short in other ways. Teachers reported that aside from a twice-yearly lecture or workshop, they usually did not take part in meaningful, ongoing, and discipline-based sessions (Stodolsky et al., 2006). "PD in my school," reported a sixth-grade teacher, "is one-size-fits-all. Early childhood teachers need specialized workshops related to their student's needs, as do I as an upper-level teacher."

* * *

Vignette #3: When a school administrator was confronted with the observation that PD opportunities were sparse, spread out, often inconsistent, and without a theme over the school year, and that topics for PD were developed primarily by administrators with little, if any, input from teachers, the response was the following: "Well, you know, finding time for our teachers to be free for such work is very difficult as they have commitments before and after school, . . . besides, we find workshops by outside consultants to be of marginal value at best. We make sure we hire very competent teachers who will need a minimum of extra PD."

Some false assumptions made by this statement are:

1. PD is useless (thus, not valued).
2. Successful teachers do not necessarily need PD.

Learning Activity #6

What is your reaction to the comment made by the school administrator above? Are the comments made well-founded? What's your view about the way PD should be offered?

_____

_____

SUPERVISION: FINDINGS AND EXPERIENCES FROM THE FIELD

Supervision

Supervision in many schools is traditional, consisting of walk-throughs and occasional formal evaluative observations without utilizing the latest cutting-edge practices in supervision. There is little evidence of professional growth plans created collaboratively between teachers and supervisors. Supervision as inspection characterizes the tone of supervisory practices in many schools. Supervision of instruction needs to be the focus of school improvement (Zepeda, 2017).

Teachers who were surveyed rarely reported positive and useful experiences during a supervisory encounter. One representative teacher stated quite bluntly, "I receive little feedback from the superiors about my teaching performance. The little feedback I do receive isn't very helpful." At another extreme, several respondents said, "My principal doesn't even pop in; he's too busy."

Evidence indicates that no structured supervisory program is employed in many schools. No written and collaboratively developed criteria for good teaching exist. Specific and disseminated criteria for good teaching need to be developed. Supervision is informal as is evaluation. Conversations among faculty with the administration should occur around questions such as, "What makes a good teacher?" "How does one recognize good teaching?" "What is the role of wait time in good teaching?" and "How do we check for student understanding continually?" etc. Further, the school should incorporate the latest technologies in supervision, introducing teachers to them and discussing their benefits.

Teachers requested to end the "dog-pony" approach to classroom observations that utilize traditional supervisory approaches in which teachers are notified in advance of an observation, then prepare their "best" lesson for a supervisor to observe, followed by a postconference and a written letter that highlights good teaching practices and needed improvements. Such approaches do not seriously encourage instructional dialogue and reflection. At the other end of the spectrum, short "walk-through" visits that offer little in-depth understandings of teaching are similarly unproductive. This is not to say that visiting classrooms is unwarranted. Supervisors must demonstrate their commitment to teaching excellence by visiting the classroom often and being available to teachers as resources.

* * *

Vignette #4: When a school administrator was confronted with the observation that there appeared to be an absence of a planned supervisory program, the response was the following: "Well, you know, we always make ourselves visible in classrooms, we check lesson plans, and we offer comments (positive and constructive criticisms) to teachers after most of our visits. We do evaluate our teachers."

Some false assumptions about that comment are:

1. Supervision is about giving teachers feedback.
2. Supervision is equated with evaluation.

Learning Activity #7

What is your reaction to the comment made by the school administrator above? In what way is supervision different from evaluation? How do you offer substantive feedback to teachers about their teaching?

_____
_____

TEACHER EVALUATION: FINDINGS AND EXPERIENCES FROM THE FIELD

Evaluation

As reported from the field and reflected in the literature, teacher evaluation has, historically, served as an accountability function. In other words, teachers, especially new and untenured ones, are observed according to some predetermined criteria to evaluate their teaching effectiveness. Tenure and promotions are generally awarded based on evidence generated from these evaluative instruments.

In some cases, instruments are "homemade," so to speak. They are usually developed by local administrators according to some obscure, subjective criteria based on expectations for good teaching practices. At other times, local district or state instruments are used without any consideration of their relevance or appropriateness for use in the context in which it is intended. Since the accountability era (Fusarelli & Fusarelli, 2019), more sophisticated instruments have been created and used, although these too lack a nuanced relationship to the particular context for which it is being used.

Teachers often report that evaluation reports they receive do not in any way promote better teaching practices. As one representative teacher reported, "Everyone knows it's a game. I try to put on my best lesson with full use of instructional materials and enthusiasm. After all, I am being evaluated.

. . . Later I receive a report, usually positive. Little, if any discussion with my supervisor ensues, . . . I go back to teaching the ways I always have. . . . I do consider myself a good teacher anyway."

Although there has been advocacy in the research literature as of late to support teacher evaluation as a means of helping them improve their teaching (Hazi, 2021), evaluation, for the most part, is conducted traditionally as a contractually driven, meaningless process other than ensuring teacher basic competency for hiring and retention purposes.

***

Vignette #5: When a school administrator was confronted with the observation that there appeared to be an absence of a planned evaluation program focused on the improvement of teacher performance, the response was the following: "Well, you know, we use a formalized evaluation process via a state-derived form to determine if our teachers are competent. We administer this instrument, at least three times a year, to untenured teachers and it gives us valuable information we can use to determine whether or not we should rehire a teacher and or offer the coveted status of tenure."

Some false assumptions about this statement are:

1. Evaluation is a fair process solely due to the use of a state-derived evaluation instrument.
2. Evaluation is an unbiased means to ascertain a teacher's minimal competence.
3. Evaluation's sole purpose is to ensure accountability.

Learning Activity #8

What role does and should teacher evaluation play in your school/district? What are some other troubling issues involving evaluation or in the manner in which it is conducted? Do you think that if a school had a robust supervisory program that evaluation would be necessary? If not, why, and if so, in what way(s)?

REFERENCES

Bass, B. M. (1985). *Leadership and performance beyond expectations*. Free Press.
Benjamin, A. (2002). *Differentiated instruction: A guide for middle and high school teachers*. Eye on Education.
Benjamin, A. (2003). *Differentiated instruction: A guide for elementary teachers*. Eye on Education.
Biddle, B. J., & Raymond, A. S. (1967). *An analysis of classroom activities*. University of Missouri.
Bloom, B. (1956). *Taxonomy of educational objectives: Cognitive domain*. Addison Wesley.
Brazer, S. D., & Bauer, S. C. (2013). Preparing instructional leaders: A model. *Educational Administration Quarterly, 49*(4), 645–684. https://doi.org/10.1177/0013161X13478977
Breslow, L. (2020). *New research points to the importance of using active learning in the classroom*. MIT Faculty Newsletter. http://web.mit.edu/fnl/vol/121/breslow9.htm
Cruickshank, V. (2017). The influence of school leadership on student outcomes. *Open Journal of Social Sciences, 5*, 115–123. http://doi.org/10.4236/jss.2017.59009
Flessa, J. J. (2012). Principals as middle managers: School leadership during the implementation of primary class size reduction policy in Ontario. *Leadership and Policy in Schools, 11*(3), 325–343. http://doi.org/10.12691/education-3-12B-9
Freire, P. (1968). *Pedagogy of the oppressed*. The Free Press.
Fullan, M. (2006). *Turnaround leadership*. Jossey-Bass.
Fullan, M. (2008). *The six secrets of change*. Jossey-Bass.
Fusarelli, L. D., & Fusarelli, B. C. (2019). Instructional supervision in an era of high-stakes accountability. In S. J. Zepeda & J. A. Ponticell (Eds.), *The Wiley handbook of educational supervision* (pp. 131–155). Wiley Blackwell.
Glanz, J. (2016). *ENGAGE: Teach, don't just present*. Motivational Press.
Glanz, J., Shaked, H., Rabinowitz, C., Shenhav, S., & Zaretsky, R. (2017). Instructional leadership practices among principals in Israeli and USA Jewish schools. *International Journal of Educational Reform, 26*(2), 132–153. https://doi.org/10.1177/105678791702600203
Goldring, E., Grissom, J. A., Neumerski, C. M., Murphy, J., Blissett, R., & Porter, A. (2015). *Making time for instructional leadership*. https://wallacefoundation.org/sites/default/files/2023-10/Making-Time-for-Instructional-Leadership-Vol-1.pdf
Hallinger, P., & Lee, M. (2013). Mapping instructional leadership in Thailand: Has education reform impacted principal practice? *Educational Management Administration and Leadership, 42*(1), 6–29. http://doi.org/10.1177/1741143213502196
Hattie, J., & Timperley, H. (2007). The power of feedback. *Review of Educational Research, 77*(1), 81–112. https://www.jstor.org/stable/4624888
Hayes, R., & Matusov, E. (2005). Designing for dialogue in place of teacher talk and student silence. *Culture and Psychology, 11*(3), 339–357. https://doi.org/10.1177/1354067X05055525

Hazi, H. M. (2021). A swerve in times of crises: Rethinking teacher evaluation anew. In J. Glanz (Ed.), *Crisis and pandemic leadership: Implications for meeting the needs of students, teachers, and parents* (pp. 47–58). Rowman & Littlefield.

Hitt, D. H. (2011). School leadership and student achievement: The mediating effects of teacher beliefs. *Educational Administration Quarterly, 47*(3), 462–494. https://doi.org/10.2307/20054196

Hoetker, J., & Ahlbrand, W. P., Jr. (1969). The persistence of the recitation. *American Education Research Journal, 6*, 145–167. http://www.jstor.org/stable/1161891

House, R. J. (1976). A theory of charismatic leadership. In J. G. Hunt & L. L. Larson (Eds.), *Leadership: The cutting edge* (pp. 189–207). Southern Illinois University Press.

Joyce, B. R., & Weil, M. (2008). *Models of teaching* (8th ed.). Allyn and Bacon.

Leithwood, K. A., &. Jantzi, D. (2005). Transformational leadership. In B. Davies (Ed.), *The essentials of school leadership* (pp. 31–43). Corwin.

Loveless, T. (2016, March 24). *Principals as instructional leaders: An international perspective*. Brookings. https://www.brookings.edu/research/principals-as-instructional-leaders-an-international-perspective/

Northouse, P. G. (2003). *Leadership: Theory and practice.* Sage.

OECD. (2022). *Education at a glance 2022.* OECD Publishing.

Sergiovanni, T. J. (2005). *Leadership for the schoolhouse: How is it different? Why is it important?* Jossey-Bass.

Shaked, H. (2018). Why principals sidestep instructional leadership: The disregarded question of schools' primary objective. *Journal of School Leadership, 28*(4), 517–538. https://doi.org/10.1177/105268461802800404

Shaked, H. (2021a). Perceptions of Israeli school principals regarding the knowledge needed for instructional leadership. *Educational Management Administration & Leadership, 51*(3). https://doi.org/10.1177/17411432211006092

Shaked, H. (2021b). Relationship-based instructional leadership. *International Journal of Leadership in Education.* https://doi.org/10.1080/13603124.2021.1944673

Shaked, H., Schechter, C., & Daly, A. J. (Eds.). *Leading holistically: How schools, districts, and states improve systematically.* Routledge.

Shava, G., & Heystek, J. (2021). Managing teaching and learning: Integrating instructional and transformational leadership in South African schools context. *International Journal of Educational Management, 35*(5), 1048–1062. https://doi.org/10.1108/IJEM-11-2020-0533

Snyder, K. J., & Snyder, K. M. (Eds.). (2023). *Systems thinking for sustainable schooling: A mindshift for educators to lead and achieve quality schools.* Rowman & Littlefield.

Stodolsky, S. S. (1981). The recitation persists, but what does it look like? *Journal Curriculum Studies, 13*(2), 121–130. https://doi.org/10.1080/0022027810130206

Sullivan, S., & Glanz, J. (2006). *Building effective learning communities: Strategies for leadership, learning, and collaboration.* Corwin.

Tanner, D., & Tanner, L. (2006). *Curriculum development: Theory into practice.* Prentice Hall.

Tedla, B. A., & Kilango, C. (2022). The role of leadership toward improving student's achievement: A case study of secondary schools in Changchuan. *Journal of Positive School Psychology, 6*(4), 6744–6755. https://journalppw.com

Tomlinson, C. (2001). Differentiated instruction in the regular classroom: What does it mean? How does it look? *Understanding Our Gifted, 14*(1), 3–6. https://eric.ed.gov/?id=EJ639193

Tomlinson, C. (2005). This issue. *Theory Into Practice, 44*(3), 183–184. http://doi.org/10.1207/s15430421tip4403_1

Wiles, J. W. (2008). *Leading curriculum development.* Corwin.

Yendol-Hoppey, D., & Fichtman-Dana, N. (2010). *Powerful professional development: Building expertise within the four walls of your school.* Corwin.

Zepeda, S. J. (2017). *Instructional supervision: Applying tools and concepts.* Routledge.

NOTES

1. The study, still ongoing, will be hopefully published in a peer-reviewed journal. As of this date, over 35 interviews with school leaders (primarily principals) have occurred, and over 100 responses from five countries have been received to the questionnaire in Appendix A.

2. Note that frontal teaching is not necessarily a negative practice. In fact, it is quite a viable approach when used appropriately among other teaching models such as jigsaw, role-playing, reciprocal teaching, inquiry-based learning, synectics, induction, etc. See discussion of "direct instruction" by Joyce and Weil (2008) in their classic book *Models of Teaching.*

Chapter 2

The Key Component of Instructional Quality

The Instructional Core

This chapter highlights extant research on practices that promote instructional quality in a school. It introduces and explains the Instructional Core (IC; termed by City et al., 2009) and that attention to it is required to achieve instructional excellence. Each component will be explicated with classroom examples and scenarios that reflect it in practice. Examples will be provided in which the IC is ignored and contrast it with best practices in which IC is *properly employed.*

FOCUS QUESTIONS

1. How would you respond when asked, "From the perspective of a classroom teacher who aims to promote student learning, what single factor is most essential to ensure instructional excellence?" (Parenthetically, certainly, teachers need to possess the requisite content knowledge as well as the ability to empathize and care for students, but this question is aimed at the technical aspects of the teaching process itself.)
2. What does the term "Instructional Core" mean to you?
3. What key steps or activities can teachers take and employ that will promote student learning?
4. What is the connection between teaching and curriculum?
5. What are the best (and worst) practices in professional development (PD), supervision, and teacher evaluation?

Carl Glickman (2020), a noted educational reformer, once astutely commented, and I paraphrase, "The reason everyone goes into education is to have a powerful influence on the educational lives of students." Those uniquely talented individuals who aspire to school leadership sincerely want to make a difference. They realize that they are in an optimal position to effect great change and provide for the larger "good." They are driven by an unyielding commitment to facilitate the conditions necessary to foster high achievement for all students (Sergiovanni, 1996). As managers, advocates, planners, mentors, supervisors, and above all else leaders, they establish a conducive tone in a school building that serves to promote educational excellence at all levels (Warwick, 2014). School administrators and supervisors (headmasters, deans, subject matter specialists, teacher leaders, principals, or assistant/associate principals) realize that for students to excel, an instructional program must be established that is rigorous, sustained, meaningful, and aligned with best practices in the field (Duignan, 2022).

Not too long ago, a principal, as "the" school leader in a particular building, was largely responsible for ensuring a safe school building, managing bus schedules, keeping order by enforcing school policies, developing master schedules, ordering books and supplies, and other logistical managerial tasks (Adams & Muthiah, 2020). According to Paul Young (2004), "That principalship doesn't exist anymore" (p. 50). Though still accountable for these and other managerial tasks (Benoliel, 2017; Glanz, 2021), principals today are ultimately responsible for providing top quality instructional leadership that aims to promote best practices in teaching and related instructional areas for the chief purpose of ensuring student personal growth and achievement (Shaked, 2022).

This emphasis on instructional improvement is clearly reflected in the burgeoning literature on school reform (Barth et al., 2005; Fullan, 2009; Hargreaves, 2022). Fullan et al. (2006) has underscored the critical importance of high-quality instruction and its systematic delivery as most necessary to ensure "continuous improvement and ongoing academic success" (p. 8). Educational researchers have demonstrated that attention to instruction, primarily, is the most important responsibility of a school leader (Shaked, 2021).

However, extant research and anecdotal evidence indicate that many schools have been unaffected by these cutting-edge practices in instructional leadership (Aureada, 2021; Carraway & Young, 2014). For instance, advances in instructional supervision have been advocated in the literature for some time (Glickman et al., 2017), yet supervision in many schools is still performed perfunctorily, utilizing traditional methods of evaluative supervision and episodic utilization of PD (Garman, 2020). Research indicates that such practices do not encourage change in teacher behavior that results in student achievement (Heaven & Bourne, 2016; Hou et al., 2019; Nettles & Herrington, 2007). The central theme of *Creating a Culture of Excellence* is to underscore the vital role of principals and their assistants (and others) to promote student learning (academic, social, interpersonal, etc.) by promoting instructional quality. Bridging the perennial divide between research and practice is the goal of this book.

CENTRAL ASSUMPTIONS ABOUT INSTRUCTIONAL LEADERSHIP AND KEY TASKS OF INSTRUCTIONAL LEADERS

The following assumptions, drawn from extant research, underscore the importance and vitality of instructional leadership:

- The principal is *the* key player in the school building to promote student learning. It's not that students cannot learn without a principal, for teachers are certainly most essential as front-line educators in the classroom. But a specially-prepared instructional leader serving as building principal is vital to accomplish deep, sustained, and school-wide achievement for all students (Leithwood et al., 2020; Neumerski, 2013).
- High achievement for all students should be the major goal for a principal (Covert, 2004; NASSP, 2013; Xu, 2018). A principal may possess charisma, increase parental participation in school activities, raise funds for the PTA, interact well with the school board, organize meaningful cultural events, or even possess great vision. However, the bottom line is that a principal, first and foremost, should be concerned with activities that actively promote good teaching that in turn promotes student learning. A principal cannot be considered successful unless high student achievement in academic areas is achieved for all students (Allensworth & Hart, 2018; Blasé & Blasé, 2000; Day et al., 2016). Parenthetically, principals certainly also support and encourage student behavioral, emotional, and social growth (Okilwa & Barnett, 2023).
- Although other forms of leadership (i.e., cultural, managerial, human resources, strategic, external development, and micropolitical) are important (Mid-Continent Research for Education and Learning [MCREL], 2001; Waters & Grubb, 2004), instructional leadership should rarely, if ever, be delegated to others. Others serve as instructional leaders for certain, but the principal plays an active and orchestrating role (Catano & Stronge, 2006).
- The effective principal is knowledgeable and skillful in the art and science of instructional supervision and leadership (Marzano, 2018).

Vignette #1: I recall my first several years of teaching in an urban elementary school. The principal had an excellent reputation as an administrator. He was well-organized, prompt, and efficient. He prided himself on his meticulous reports that were distributed to officials in the district office. He was not, however, an instructional leader.

He taught for about four years before assuming his first administrative position as an assistant principal. Within a few years he was promoted to principal. His organizational and interpersonal skills brought him notoriety. I recall that he was an avid runner. Although he didn't run marathons, he was adept at LSD, that is, long slow distance runs. We shared many a conversation about running since, at the time, I too was into LSD. We usually conversed about aspects of running from the shoes we wore to where we ran. These conversations took place while waiting to take my class up to the classroom during morning lineup. We never spoke about teaching or about what I was doing to promote student achievement. He didn't, it seemed to me, feel comfortable talking about teaching. After all, he had only been a teacher for a short time. His forte was administration. He believed that a good principal sets a conducive tone in a school building so as to allow teachers to "do their thing," as he used to say back in the '70s. His philosophy was to foster good student discipline, a well-run school, and to leave instruction to teachers.

As a new teacher, I yearned to talk to someone about my instructional practices. Although the district reading supervisor occasionally popped in, our conversations were usually brief. As a new teacher, I had to learn through trial and error. Those poor kids during my early years of teaching were victims of my instructional experiments.

It was several years later when I was transferred to another school that I realized how valuable a supervisor can be as an instructional leader. Mr. Chiradelli, our assistant principal, was not only well-organized and personable but he also was comfortable about talking to us about teaching. He was the first assistant principal who actually said to me, "Jeffrey, no, let me show you." On the spot, he demonstrated good pedagogical practice by taking over my class to show me how to more effectively pose critical thinking questions and check for understanding. Seeing a model in action, I was uplifted. Mr. Chiradelli was a teacher of teachers and a very effective assistant principal.

Learning Activity #1

Record your reaction to Vignette 1 and share your experiences.

_____

_____

More specifically, extant research indicates that effective instructional leaders understand the following:

1. The single greatest influence on students in a classroom is the teacher. "Teachers have a powerful, long-lasting influence on their students" (Stronge, 2018, p. vii). Good principals support good teachers by providing instructional services and resources on a continuing basis (Karacabey, 2021). Moreover, good principals attract and hire certified teachers who have specific knowledge, skills, and dispositions that are essential to promote student achievement; certified teachers are more successful than unlicensed teachers (Darling-Hammond, 2008). Good principals also realize that retaining good teachers is essential because experience counts. "Experienced teachers differ from rookie teachers in that they have attained expertise through real-life experiences, classroom practice, and time" (Stronge, 2018, p. 9). Research demonstrates that teachers with more experience plan better, apply a range of teaching strategies, understand students' learning needs, and better organize instruction. Good principals appreciate the importance of this research.
2. An emphasis on academics is crucial. Effective principal instructional leaders spend much time discussing the instructional program with colleagues, teachers, parents, students, and lay leaders. They spend all available time discussing instruction: personal informal and formal contacts with teachers, memoranda, email communications, grade and faculty conferences, assembly programs, parent meetings, etc. (Horng et al., 2010). They realize that establishing an orderly environment conducive to educational excellence is necessary. Good principals set high expectations and standards for success (Pont et al., 2008).

More specifically related to instructional improvement, effective principals:

- develop, in collaboration with teachers, clear and consistent school-wide instructional policies;
- ensure that instructional time is protected (e.g., good principals ensure that intrusions are kept to a minimum, that is, excessive announcements over the loudspeaker, intrusionary attendance report collection by office monitors, etc.—all of which interrupts and compromises classroom teaching and learning);
- examine instructional grouping patterns to ensure student mastery of content;
- establish clearly defined academic goals for the school (by grade);
- facilitate a process to develop and revise curriculum in all content areas;
- involve teachers in curriculum planning and decision-making;
- maintain systematic methods of assessment;
- review data collected as a result of implementation of an assessment system;

- share and use the data to help improve the instructional school program;
- observe teachers and students engaged in the learning process;
- assist teachers who are having instructional difficulties;
- provide opportunities for teachers to learn and professionally grow; and
- provide for meaningful and ongoing collaboratively-developed professional development opportunities.

Vignette #2: One of the most impressive schools I have been fortunate to visit was International High School (IHS), a multicultural alternative educational environment for recent arrivals, serving students with varying degrees of limited English proficiency. The innovative principal Eric Nadelstern, widely known at the time, organized the school as interdisciplinary teams. On each team, four teachers (math, science, English, and social studies) and a support services coordinator were jointly responsible for a heterogeneous group of about 75 9th- through 12th-grade students. The faculty worked with the same group of students for a full year providing a complete academic program organized around themes such as "Motion" or "The American Dream." Teams also provided effective academic counseling.

The interdisciplinary team concept provided an ideal infrastructure for significant opportunities for PD, power over curriculum, allocating resources, and even budgeting and scheduling. Time was built into their schedules by the principal for meetings to do many of the bulleted items described above. Team teaching, flexible grouping, and block scheduling were frequently employed. Teams developed peer observations and spent much time in and out of each other's classrooms discussing instructional practices.

Dr. Nadelstern saw his role as a means for establishing a school-wide focus on teaching and learning, building a powerful community of leaders and learning, modeling interactions with teachers of the kind of relationships they should develop with students, developing a collegial vision and purpose, serving as a resource for solving problems, etc.

Learning Activity #2

Describe the ways you have seen school leaders establish a culture of teaching and learning.

---

3. The three primary elements of successful instructional leadership (Blasé & Blasé, 2004), more specifically, are:

a. Conducting instructional conferences: Whether involved in pre- or post-observation conferences, informal or more formal grade conferences, etc. effective principals, according to Blasé and Blasé (2004), make suggestions, give feedback, model, use inquiry, and solicit opinions from teachers.
b. Providing staff development: According to Blasé and Blasé (2004), "Behaviors associated with providing staff development include emphasizing the study of teaching and learning, support for collaboration, development of coaching relationships, use of action research, provision of resources, and application of the principles of adult growth and development to all phases of the staff development program" (p. 162).
c. Developing teacher reflection: Effective principals purposefully engage teachers in articulating feelings, sharing attitudes, and deep thinking about instructional issues (Darling-Hammond et al., 2022).

Vignette #3: The following principals' comments are not representative of school leaders as a whole, but his comments do indicate an ignorance of extant best practices.

I once visited a high school in Los Angeles, California. A friend I had known in college, but had not seen in 30 years, was the new principal. We began reminiscing about college but then the conversation turned "pedagogical." I discussed my research and work on teaching, supervision, and my vision for good schooling when he suddenly interrupted and assertively stated, "Now Jeffrey, you don't believe that garbage do you? 'Professional learning communities,' give me a break. Did we have them when we were in high school? We turned out pretty damn good, didn't we? I learned history and math primarily through memorization and I was able to tie things together using my own faculties. We rarely had PD. We knew how to think on our feet. This teaching thing, you know, is all intuitive. If I had a question, I'd ask a colleague . . . no need for meeting after meeting. I agree, though," continuing his tirade, "teachers today are really a sad lot; they are ill-prepared, . . . don't even know their content; I have to spoon feed them. There's no discipline in this school and I don't mean the kids. I have to run a tight ship, . . . be tough with teachers; they have to know who's the boss." He later admitted that he "had spewed forth this 'pedagogical correctness' about involving teachers, inviting greater parental involvement, building team spirit, etc. during the interviews because he knew "what the committee wanted to hear" but that while he espoused such views, he didn't believe in them and, certainly, didn't act on them.

30   *Chapter 2*

Learning Activity #3

What do you think my response was to him? How would you have responded? Share your reactions with a colleague.

_____

_____

INSTRUCTIONAL QUALITY WITHIN A PROFESSIONAL LEARNING COMMUNITY: A THEORETICAL FRAMEWORK FOR CREATING AND SUSTAINING EXCELLENCE

Instructional quality, as best practice, is a school-wide process in which teaching and learning become the core of the school's mission. Principals and other administrators work to develop a professional learning community that supports such work (Miller, 2020). A professional learning community has five dimensions:

1. Supportive and shared leadership (e.g., school administrators participate democratically with teachers sharing power, authority, and decision making).
2. Shared values and vision (e.g., the principal or head and staff decide on the values and vision of the school and support its realization).
3. Collective learning (e.g., staff and the administration come together to learn how best to improve student performance).
4. Supportive conditions (e.g., principals and teachers possess adequate resources to promote instructional excellence and create structures that facilitate learning for all).

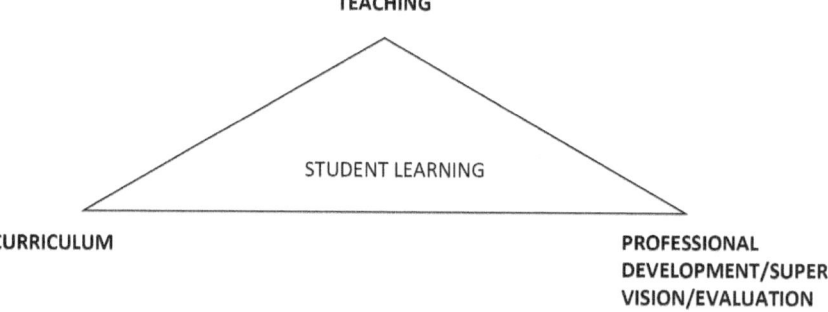

Figure 2.1. The tripod view of instructional quality in a school.

5. Shared personal practice (e.g., peer review and feedback are school norms as is feedback given to administrators by teachers in informal and formal ways).

Instructional leaders within professional learning communities keep instructional quality as their focus.

To provide a theoretical frame for discussion of instructional quality (as measured by student learning), see Figure 2.1, which highlights the key components of instruction: teaching, curriculum, professional development, supervision, and evaluation. Instructional quality is achieved through excellent teaching, facilitated by cutting-edge practices in professional development, and an articulated and deep understanding of the content skills and values embedded in the curriculum. Further, best practices in supervision and evaluation lend credence and support for a vibrant instructional program.

Vignette #4: Much of the work during my career has been to conduct instructional quality audits of schools. I am frequently invited by the school administration (sometimes at the behest of the school board) to conduct such a review. For the audit, I do not use a checklist or prescribed format. Rather, after speaking with school officials, I tailor-make the audit based on needs articulated by school officials. I look at teaching practices, PD (including supervision and evaluation procedures or processes), and the state of curriculum development. I interview all constituents, including all administrators, a representative sample of teachers, staff, parents, lay leaders, and students. I also request to view all instructional documents, including test data and analyses. A good part of my time is spent observing many classrooms at all grade levels and subjects. I then write my report and share it with school leaders. Based on my report and their perceptions of its relevance and accuracy, they develop an action plan in each of the three areas: teaching, curriculum, and PD (see Appendix K for a sample action plan chart or more formally called The Instructional Goals Matrix). A short excerpt of a report I wrote while serving as a consultant that does not reflect any one particular school (done to ensure anonymity) but rather a compilation of several different schools is presented here:

Although the report details specific recommendations with suggested guidelines, following is a list of areas of concern:

- *Frontal teaching*—Despite the small class sizes and use of Smart Boards, frontal teaching is the dominant model utilized. With the exception of one class, all others had students sitting in rows. Recitation was evident in all situations wherein the teacher was most active, guiding lessons, posing questions, in rapid succession and calling randomly upon selected students. Several students during choral recitals (i.e., repeating in unison words or phrases uttered by the teacher first) and during whole class instruction were off-task, either on the wrong page, working slowly on a project, or simply not engaged. The teacher's attention was focused on approximately 50 percent of the students of the class with many students' educational needs not attended to, a common problem with overuse of frontal teaching. Although the school does not track classes, observations of teaching in most classes indicate that teachers teach to the average, missing out on those gifted learners, while not attending sufficiently to the needs of struggling students. Teachers need PD on an ongoing basis in differentiated instruction. Such an approach will enable teachers to more effectively and consistently address the learning needs of all students during a given lesson. Additional ongoing, consistent, and collaboratively developed PD is needed to assist educators with the latest pedagogical approaches including, for instance, proper use of wait time, formative assessment strategies, individualized approaches to teaching, including differentiated instruction. I did not see, in my class visits, much use of formative assessment strategies or checking for understanding.

- *Curriculum development*—Development of curriculum needs more ongoing, comprehensive attention, although a start has been made in the areas of science and social studies in alignment with state curricular guidelines. The mere existence of these standards, however, does not imply that curriculum development is occurring. Curriculum development involves deep and ongoing conversations collaboratively refined by both administrators and teachers. End of year conversations should take place among teachers regarding the effectiveness of the curriculum. Teachers at different grade levels rarely converse over curricular issues. Teachers at the school need ongoing conversations about curriculum to ensure proper articulation. Administrators need to provide time for teachers to converse over the curriculum.
- *Professional development*—PD in the school is relegated to a few minutes each month at monthly faculty meetings. These meetings, by and large, focus on administrative announcements. The district does occasionally require teachers to attend bi-monthly PD workshops, but these sessions are not ongoing, differentiated, nor relevant to the needs of a lot of teachers in the school, as reported by teachers in my interviews with them. Further, after perusing the school's budget, I couldn't locate a budget line for PD. The principal told me, "Yes, it's there." I looked again but could not locate it. He then pointed to the line that read "Misc."

- *Supervision and evaluation*—Supervision at the school is traditional, too informal, and lacks consistency of use. The administrators could use additional professional development in the latest approaches related to cutting edge practices in supervision. Supervision of instruction needs to be the focus of school improvement. Supervision and evaluation are confused. Teacher evaluation at the school is contractually driven and administrators utilize a form, based on Charlette Danielson's (2007) four domains for teacher competency. The form itself merely lists her four categories with a few descriptors and without a precise explanation for what satisfactory, unsatisfactory, or stellar performance looks like. Comments made by evaluators are subjective. There is no indication that such evaluations change teaching behavior or improve instruction. It does, however, serve an accountability function and contractual obligation. Most teachers shared their ambivalence with this "dog and pony" type observation. One representative teacher stated, "I'd rather them just pop in my room anytime rather than have to put on a meaningless show for them."

See Appendix F for a Teacher's Self-Assessment Questionnaire that can be completed and discussed with a supervisor or colleague to provoke instructional dialogue about the practice of teaching. Such dialogue is crucial and much more meaningful than traditional approaches to supervision and evaluation.

Learning Activity #4

What is your reaction to Vignette #4? Share your experiences. Do your experiences corroborate with any of the findings mentioned above? Explain.

_____

_____

Learning Activity #5

This might be a good time to fill out some of the questionnaires found in the appendices (i.e., A, D, E, F, G, and H), depending on your position in the school. Jot down some of your reactions or reflections based on your own experiences in taking and sharing the questionnaires with others.

_____

_____

Vignette #5: Not too long ago I visited a high school in the northeast. I was to observe a student teacher. In discussions with the cooperating teacher, he mentioned to me that he is rarely given any feedback on his teaching. "They do, you know, that 'dog and pony' routine. I'm told I'll be observed on a certain date and time. There's no time for a preconference, but I'm told, reluctantly I sense, that if I insist on one my department chair will make the time for it. I'm observed for about 25 minutes of the 50-minute period and given a post conference a week later that lasts about five minutes. Then two weeks later a letter summarizing the observation miraculously appears in my mailbox. I perfunctorily sign and submit it . . . over and done with. . . . I learn nothing new about my teaching." I asked him about PD in the school and I am told that the two days allotted for it before the school year were "taken away due to budget cuts." "We have two other days, one in the fall and spring semesters, but they are a waste of time." I queried for more information, and he tells me that the PD offered is not related to his discipline (science) and that the presenter usually hasn't set foot in a high school classroom in a decade, if at all. "We are never asked for what we really need and want." When asked about time spent in instructional dialogue with supervisors or fellow teachers, he replies, "My principal does talk with me but not about teaching; he loves basketball and he knows I do too, so when meet all we talk about is the latest game or the Miami Heat's LeBron James."

Learning Activity #6

What is your reaction to Vignette #5? Share your experiences. Are the comments made by this educator exaggerated?

_____
_____

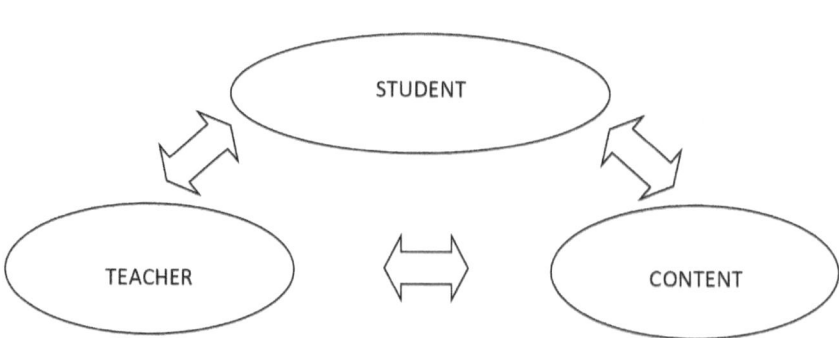

Figure 2.2. The Instructional Core.

In Chapter 3, I will amplify each of these areas of concern as they relate to a school's instructional quality.

Figure 2.1, however, is inadequate by itself to fully comprehend the import of the instructional process without turning attention to a deeper level of the instructional process: called the "Instructional Core" (see City et al., 2009). The Instructional Core (see Figure 2.2) is "composed of the teacher and the student in the presence of the content" (p. 22). A reciprocal relationship exists between each component (i.e., between student and teacher, teacher and student, student and content, and teacher and content). City et al. (2009) explain:

> Simply stated, the instructional task is the actual work that students are asked to do in the process of instruction—*not* [italics in original] what teachers *think* they are asking students to do, or what the official curriculum *says* . . . , but what they are *actually* doing. (p. 23)

Learning occurs in the interaction among these three vital components. For instance, if we match the level of content to the students' ability level, then learning is more likely to occur. As teachers' knowledge of the content and skills in delivering it increases, students are more likely to learn. If students themselves are engaged in learning (e.g., on task, challenged, monitored), then learning is more likely to occur than without such attention to student engagement. City et al. (2009) say it plainly: "If you are not doing one of these three things, you are not improving instruction and learning (p. 24).

It is important to emphasize that the structures we employ to encourage learning (e.g., learning communities, differentiation, grouping, supervision, block scheduling, individualization, instructional prompts, professional development, etc.) do not, by and in themselves, improve learning. Rather, these structures must influence the instructional core for learning to occur. For example, if professional development is aimed at changing teacher behavior in the classroom and appropriate follow-up is employed to help the teacher gain a better understanding of the two other elements of the instructional core (students and content), then learning will be enhanced (Johnson & Fargo, 2010). City et al. (2009) explain:

> At the very best, when they are working well, they *create conditions* that influence what goes on inside the instructional core. The primary work of schooling occurs inside the classrooms, *not* in the organizations and institutions that surround the classroom. Schools don't improve through political and managerial incantation; they improve through the complex and demanding work of teaching and learning. (p. 25)

More pointedly, whether we are employing supervision, professional development, or any of the other structures, activities, or processes that impact teacher behavior and student learning, four questions in the instructional process (City et al., 2009, p. 27) must be always considered:

1. How will this affect teachers' knowledge and skills?
2. How will this affect the level of content in classrooms?
3. How will this affect the role of the student in the instructional process?
4. How will this affect the relationship between [and among] the teacher, the student, and content?

When teachers are observed by peers or supervisors, the observer can tell if learning occurred by examining the instructional core and ask (City et al., 2009, p. 88):

1. What are the teachers doing and saying?
2. What are the students doing and saying (in response to teacher behavior)?
3. What is the task?

Consider the next vignette.

Vignette #6: Joshua, a seventh grader at Wakefield Middle School, is asked to join a cooperative learning group with three other students to solve some math problems. Ms. Reynolds, Joshua's teacher, circulates among the students making sure all groups are on task and fully understand the assignment. Joshua, a shy, usually withdrawn child listens as his group tackles the math problems. Joshua's group is the first to complete all the problems. As they wait for Ms. Reynolds to review the problems with the class they take out their readers. Ms. Reynolds notices that the group is finished, and she asks them, "Have you reviewed each problem carefully?" to which they all nod in the affirmative. Joshua goes along but remains clueless.

In Vignette #6, Ms. Reynolds did not note, at least in this situation, that the level of the *content* was too difficult for Joshua as he had not yet mastered some basic mathematical computation skills necessary to solve most of the problems. Secondly, Ms. Reynolds, the *teacher*, was more concerned with the managerial aspects of coordinating multiple cooperative learning groups than she was with attending to individual learning needs of some students. Lastly, Joshua, the *student*, was not actively engaged in working with his partners; he was a passive observer. The essence of teaching involves paying attention to the relationship among the level of *content*, the *teacher*'s skill and knowledge she brings to the teaching of that content, and the need to ensure that the *student* is actively learning the content with the teacher's guidance, if necessary.

The supervisor also needs to pay attention to the Instructional Core. Notice in this next vignette the advice Mr. Goldstein, the assistant principal, gives Ms. Reynolds in the post conference after having observed her cooperative learning math lesson above.

Vignette #7:

> Mr. Goldstein: *Thank you for inviting me to observe this wonderful lesson. The students appeared on task, and you continually circulated to ensure proper adherence to effective classroom management. I noticed no fooling around during the entire lesson. Good job. How do you think the lesson went?*
>
> Ms. Reynolds: *Yes, thanks. I thought the lesson went as planned. I wanted to build rapport among the students through cooperative learning as well as help them reinforce the mathematical concepts they learned over the past several weeks. Do you have any suggestions for me?*
>
> Mr. Goldstein: *Well, you are a very good teacher as your organizational skills are superior. I haven't seen as good a classroom manager as you in a long time. I would, however, make a few suggestions for your consideration: One, instead of handing out the math papers yourself why not designate an individual from each group to do so? Two, it's important to not only write the objective on the board, as you did, but to also indicate the math standard you are addressing. Three, in reviewing the math problems, I might suggest you call on group volunteers at random rather than go in sequential order from one end of the room to the other . . . you know, keep the kids on their toes.*

Aside from the ineffective supervisory approach taken by Mr. Goldstein, which will be addressed in Chapter 3, he does not pay attention to the Instructional Core. None of his suggestions, even if Ms. Reynolds follows them, will substantively improve her teaching and better promote learning.

Learning Activity #7

Can you think of a scenario in which a supervisor might better guide the conversation so that the instructional core is addressed more effectively?

Look at this next scenario in contrast to Vignette #7.

Vignette #8: I was privileged to visit a master supervisor at an elementary school in the southern part of the United States who adeptly helped a teacher focus on what really matters about teaching: the Instructional Core. Although

I didn't take notes at the time (wish I had recorded the incident), the following is my version of the interaction between this assistant principal and a new teacher during a postconference (feedback session):

S: *Hi Helen. I'm happy we have this time to discuss your lesson.*

T: *Yes, I am very interested in hearing your reactions and offering me some suggestions for improvement.*

S: *Well Helen, you do recall that when we met during the preconference I asked you to identify some areas of interest that you wanted me to focus on. We agreed that I'd look at your use of questions throughout the lesson. Although we didn't use any particular format or instrument to record the questions you asked, I did have the opportunity to take pretty careful notes at various points in your lesson. Perhaps we can start at that point for our discussion?*

T: *Sounds fine with me*

S: *Great, I had some time to write out this question-answer sequence between you and a few students. Why don't you take a look at it now and tell me if you feel I accurately recorded the transaction and, even more importantly, what it may mean to you about your teaching? [Supervisor shares a one page dialogue with the teacher that also included a make-shift seating chart with some arrows indicating who was asking the question, what the question was, who responded and to whom, and what was said.]*

[A few minutes pass as the teacher reads and reflects on the data]

T: *Umm . . . interesting. I notice my questions are succinct and, I think well-phrased . . . students seem to have responded.*

S: *Yes, your questions were well put and relevant to the lesson. Can you perhaps take a look at to whom you were speaking and describe the manner in which they responded?*

T: *I see I must have called on (mentions names of students).*

S: *Can you see anything in common about their seating location?*

T: *Well, they are all seated near my desk. [Supervisor shows teacher three other illustrations of conversations with a similar pattern.] I didn't really realize I was focusing only on a handful of students [four] seated near my desk. You know, you get caught up in conveying info that sometimes you're not cognizant, you know.*

S: *Certainly.*

T: *I also notice the arrows you drew indicate that each student responds directly back to me after my question.*

S: *So, what could that indicate about your teaching?*

T: *I control conversations by having them only talk to me? [Thinks] Maybe I could encourage students to react to each other's comments as well?*

S: *Why would that be beneficial?*

T: *I'd be involving more students in the lesson . . . and, uh . . .*

S: *I think you're right. What do you notice about each student's response to your questions?*

[Pause]

T: *Well, they answer the question.*

S: *How?*

T: *Briefly, . . . quickly. [Supervisor shows teacher the same three other illustrations of conversations with a similar pattern.] I guess they're all the same.*

S: *In what way?*

T: *Brief.*

S: *Yes, what could that indicate?*

T: *I don't give them time for elaboration? [Teacher asks for a moment to think.] You know, I'm a new teacher and I get nervous sometimes. I won't cover my material so sometimes, I think, I look for the "right" answer from students and want to move on with the lesson. So I don't give students perhaps enough time to absorb or elaborate, or something.*

S: *That's a very astute and honest assessment, especially from a new teacher. I appreciate your forthrightness.*

T: *Thanks.*

S: *Sometimes many of us, even more experienced teachers do the same thing, rush to get through, don't allow enough time for students to interact with each other and really understand the material before we go on. Such a teaching pattern is commonly referred to as "recitation" in which a teacher poses a question, quickly calls on a student to respond (the response is usually a few words). Then the teacher, at times, repeats the students' response and moves on to the next question and the next student. It is quite common.*

T: *I know.*

S: *Let me ask you a question. What are other students doing during the time such recitation is going on?*

T: *I guess listening?*

S: *Perhaps. How do you know?*

T: *Well, I sense it . . . ugh, perhaps next time I'd better look around and be a bit more attentive.*

S: *We can discuss some strategies I've used to key in on the students a bit later. But let me ask you another question. What can tell me about the difficulty level of the content for this lesson?*

Let me end this scenario at this point. What can you say about the supervisor's approach in this vignette compared to the one earlier with Mr. Goldstein?

Certainly, you notice the supervisor in this recent scenario is not evaluative nor as prescriptive as was Mr. Goldstein. Although we can elaborate further on the supervisory approaches used by each supervisor, what can you say about the nature of their comments and what they tried to emphasize?

To my sense, this supervisor engaged the teacher in some reflective thinking about her lesson about key components of a particular aspect of the teaching process, that is, her use of questions. By focusing on the instructional core, this teacher is engaging in reflective dialogue with her supervisor (or it could be with another colleague) about some very critical aspect of teaching.

A major theme in *Creating a Culture of Excellence* is to urge school leaders to accentuate their role as instructional leaders by focusing the majority of their efforts on the Instructional Core. Moreover, school leaders need to accentuate their role as instructional leaders as they also balance managerial, political, financial, operational, and communal imperatives. Too many leaders eschew instructional leadership responsibilities for a variety of reasons including perceived time constraints, increase in administrative report-keeping from the central office, management of school-wide student behavioral issues, lack of knowledge on how to best engage experienced teachers in discussions about teaching practice, among others (Shaked, 2018; 2019).[1] To do so, however, is myopic and detrimental toward spearheading student academic achievement and overall social and emotional growth. The next chapter provides strategies for balancing managerial responsibilities with quality time to improve teaching in classrooms and school-wide.

REFERENCES

Adams, D., & Muthiah, V. (2020). School principals and 21st century leadership challenges: A systematic review. *Journal of Nusantara Studies, 5*(1), 189–210. https://doi.org/10.24200/jonus.vol5iss1pp189–210

Allensworth, E., & Hart, H. (2018). How do principals influence student achievement? https://consortium.uchicago.edu/sites/default/files/2018-10/Leadership%20Snapshot-Mar2018-Consortium.pdf

Aureada, J. U. (2021). The instructional leadership practices of school heads. *International Journal of Educational Management and Development Studies, 2*(2), 75–89. https://iiari.org/wp-content/uploads/2021/06/ijemds.v2.2.142.pdf

Barth, R., DuFour, DuFour, R., & Eaker, R. (2005). *On common ground: The power of professional learning communities.* Solution Tree.

Benoliel, P. (2017). Managing school management team boundaries and school improvement: An investigation of the school leader role. *International Journal of Leadership in Education, 20*(1), 57–86. https://doi.org/10.1080/13603124.2015.1053536

Blase, J., & Blase, J. (2000). Effective instructional leadership: Teachers' perspectives on how principals promote teaching and learning in schools. *Journal of Educational Administration, 38*(2), 130–141. http://dx.doi.org/10.1108/09578230010320082

Blasé, J., & Blasé, J. (2004). *Handbook of instructional leadership: How successful principals promote teaching and learning.* Corwin.

Carraway, J. H., & Young, T. (2014). Implementation of a district-wide policy to improve principals' instructional leadership: Principals' sense-making of the skillful observational and coaching laboratory. *Educational Policy, 29*(1), 230–256. http://doi.org/10.1177/0895904814564216

Catano, N., & Stronge, J. H. (2006). What are principals expected to do? Congruence between principal evaluation and performance standards. *NASSP Bulletin, 90*(3), 221–237. https://doi.org/10.1177/0192636506292211

City, E. A., Elmore, R. F., Fiarman, S. E., & Teitel, L. (2009). *Instructional rounds in education: A network approach to improving teaching and learning.* Harvard Educational Press.

Covert, S. P. (2004). Principals and student achievement: What the research says. *NASSP Bulletin, 88*(639), 92–94. https://doi.org/10.1177/019263650408863909

Danielson, C. (2007). *Enhancing professional practice: A framework for teaching* (2nd ed.). Association for Supervision and Curriculum Development.

Darling-Hammond, L. (2008). Teacher learning that supports student learning. In B. Z. Presseisen (Ed.), *Teaching for intelligence* (2nd ed.) (pp. 91–100). Corwin.

Darling-Hammond, L., Wechsler, M. E., Levin, S., Leung-Gagne, M., & Tozer, S. (2022). *Developing effective principals: What kind of learning matters?* Wallace.

Day, C., Gu, Q., & Sammons, P. (2016). The impact of leadership on student outcomes: How successful school leaders use transformational and instructional strategies to make a difference. *Educational Administration Quarterly, 52*(2), 221–258. https://doi.org/10.1177/0013161X15616863

DuFour, R., Eaker, R., & DuFour, R. (Eds.). (2005). *On common ground: The power of professional learning communities.* Solution Tree.

Duignan, P. (2022). *Leading educational systems and schools in times of disruption and exponential change: A call for courage, commitment, and collaboration.* Emerald Publishing.

Fullan, M. (Ed.). (2009). *The challenge of change: Start school improvement now.* Corwin.

Fullan, M., Hill, P., & Crevola, C. (2006). *Breakthrough.* Corwin.

Garman, N. (2020). The dream of clinical supervision: Critical perspectives on the state of supervision, and our long-lived accountability nightmare. *Journal of Educational Supervision, 3*(3). https://doi.org/10.31045/jes.3.3.2

Glanz, J. (Ed.). (2021). *Managing today's schools: New skills for school leaders in the 21st century.* Rowman & Littlefield.

Glickman, C. D., & West-Burns, R. (2020). *Leadership for learning: How to bring out the best in every teacher* (2nd ed.). Association for Supervision and Curriculum Development.

Glickman, C. D., Gordon, S. P, & Ross-Gordon, J. M. (2017). *SuperVision and instructional leadership: A developmental approach* (10th ed.). Pearson.

Hargreaves, A. (2022). High school change: A reflective essay on three decades of frustration, struggle, and progress. *Journal of Educational Administration, 60*(3), 245–261. https://www.andyhargreaves.com/uploads/5/2/9/2/5292616/hargreaves_jea_highschoolchange_may2022.pdf

Heaven, G., & Bourne, P. A. (2016). Instructional leadership and its effect on students' academic performance. *Review Public Administration Management, 4*(197). http://doi.org/10.1108/09513541111100107

Horng, E. L., Klasik, D., & Loeb, S. (2010). Principal's time use and school effectiveness. *American Journal of Education, 116*(4), 491–523. https://doi.org/10.1086/653625

Hou, Y., Cui, Y., & Zhang, D. (2019). Impact of instructional leadership on high school student academic achievement in China. *Asia Pacific Education Review, 20,* 543–558. https://doi.org/10.1007/s12564-019-09574-4

Johnson, C. C., & Fargo, J. D. (2010). Urban school reform enabled by transformative professional development: Impact on teacher change and student learning of science. *Urban Education, 45*(1), 4–29. https://doi.org/10.1177/0042085909352073

Karacabey, M. F. (2021). School principal support in teacher professional development. *International Journal of Educational Leadership and Management, 9*(1). http://dx.doi.org/10.17583/ijelm.2020.5158

Leithwood, K., Harris, A., & Hopkins, D. (2020). Seven strong claims about successful school leadership revisited. *School Leadership & Management, 40*(1), 5–22. https://doi.org/10.1080/13632434.2019.1596077

Marshall, K. (2013). *Rethinking teacher supervision and evaluation.* Jossey-Bass.

Marzano, R. (2018). *The handbook for the new art and science of teaching.* Solution Tree Press.

Mid-continent Research for Education and Learning (MCREL). (2001). *Leadership for school improvement* (Rev. ed.). Miller, A. (2020, January 3). Creating effective professional learning communities. edutopia, https://www.edutopia.org/article/creating-effective-professional-learning-communities

NASSP (National Association of Secondary School Leadership. (2013). Leadership matters: What the research says about the importance of principal leadership. https://www.naesp.org/sites/default/files/LeadershipMatters.pdf

Nettles, S. M., & Herrington, C. (2007). Revisiting the importance of the direct effects of school leadership on student achievement: The implications for school improvement policy. *Peabody Journal of Education, 82*(4), 724–36. http://www.jstor.org/stable/25594768

Neumerski, C. M. (2013). Rethinking instructional leadership, a review: What do we know about principal, teacher, and coach instructional leadership, and where should we go from here? *Educational Administration Quarterly, 49*(2), 310–47. https://doi.org/10.1177/0013161X12456700

Okilwa, N., & Barnett, B. (2023, January 27). What school principals do is crucial to students' emotional wellbeing. 360. https://360info.org/what-school-principals-do-is-crucial-to-students-emotional-wellbeing/

Pont, B., Nusche, D., & Moorman, H. (2008). *Improving school leadership.* OECD.

Sergiovanni, T. J. (1996). *Moral leadership: Getting to the heart of school improvement.* Jossey-Bass.

Shaked, H. (2018). Why principals sidestep instructional leadership: The disregarded question of schools' primary objective. *Journal of School Leadership, 28*(4), 517–538. https://haimshaked.com/wp-content/uploads/2019/07/pdf-27.pdf

Shaked, H. (2019). Perceptual inhibitors of instructional leadership in Israeli principals. *School Leadership & Management, 39*(5), 519–536. https://haimshaked.com/wp-content/uploads/2019/10/pdf.pdf

Shaked, H. (2021). Relationship-based instructional leadership. *International Journal of Leadership in Education.* http://doi.org/10.1080/13603124.2021.1944673

Shaked, H. (2022). *New explorations for instructional leaders: How principals can promote teaching and learning effectively.* Rowman & Littlefield.

Stronge, J. H. (2018). *Qualities of effective teachers* (3rd ed.). Association for Supervision and Curriculum Development.

Warwick, R. (2014). *The challenge of school leaders: A new way of thinking about leadership.* Rowman & Littlefield.

Waters, T., & Grubb, S. (2004). *The leadership we need: Using research to strengthen the use of standards for administrator preparation and licensure program.* Mid-continent Research for Education and Learning (MCREL).

Xu, X. (2018). *Principal's impact on student achievement.* Stronge & Associates.

Young, P. G. (2004). *You have to go to school—You're the principal: 101 tips to make it better for your students, your staff, and yourself.* Corwin.

NOTE

1. Some school leaders also share three characteristics (Hargreaves & Shirley, 2002 as cited by Marshall, 2013): (1) presentism—a short-term perspective that prevents them from envisioning or planning collaboratively for long-term systemic change; (2) conservatism—a mistrust of reform initiatives and a reluctance to change familiar classroom practices, even in the face of research findings and pupil learning outcomes suggesting that better approaches are needed; and (3) individualism—school leaders often work in isolation from colleagues and such isolation may result in lower levels of self-efficacy, less relational trust, and lack of awareness of other best practices. This lack of trust, parenthetically, also extends to those of us who teach at the university level. The perception is that we are not practitioners, although many of us have been former teachers and administrators, and that since we deal in "theory" we have little to offer in terms of insights into practice. Such dichotomous thinking

that theory and practice are bifurcated is myopic and imprecise. Some practitioners are ill-informed if they think that what they do in the classroom is not informed by some theory or research.

Chapter 3

An Overview of Best Practices in Teaching, Curriculum, Professional Development, Supervision, and Evaluation

This chapter outlines several key research-based strategies that enable high-quality instruction to become a dominant force in schools. Specific best practices will be reviewed in each of the five domains, as reflected in the title of this chapter.

FOCUS QUESTIONS

1. What are some of the key teaching skills necessary to promote student learning?
2. What role does curriculum play in a good instructional program, and what are some best practices for developing curriculum?
3. What have been your experiences with participating in professional development (PD), and as a leader, what are the key elements of establishing effective PD?
4. What are the best practices of instructional supervision?
5. What role does teacher evaluation play in your school, and how might the evaluative process be optimized?

PROMOTING INSTRUCTIONAL EXCELLENCE

The material that follows includes suggestions to improve a school's academic program that's in line with best practices culled from both the latest research and literature in the field of instructional quality. This chapter provides specific, concrete suggestions, with explanations of best practices in each of the following five instructional areas: teaching, curriculum development, PD, supervision, and evaluation. Please note that the information that follows is meant as an introduction because an entire volume can be written on each of these topics alone. I have selected practices that research and anecdotal evidence culled from the field indicate having the highest impact on student learning. In Appendix I, annotated references and other works are cited for readers interested in a more full treatment of the subject.

Again, the theme of *Creating a Culture of Excellence* is that a school leader who wants to promote instructional excellence must focus efforts on implementing the suggestions offered in this chapter. In Chapter 4 is a case study about a school that attempted, in its first stages, to promote instructional change and thereby transform school culture to improve teaching and learning.

One last point as mentioned in the Introduction, instructional practices are influenced by many cultural, social, economic, and even political factors. Understanding the unique context in which these and other practices are situated is necessary. Yet, as mentioned, one can indeed cull basic, even common-sense skills that transcend these differences so that educators can glean currently known best practices to promote learning in schools.[1]

AN OVERVIEW OF BEST PRACTICES IN TEACHING

Instructional leadership is about encouraging best practices in teaching. To do so requires school leaders to become familiar with innovative teaching theories and practices and encourage teachers to model them in classrooms.

The box below summarizes the teaching ideas highlighted in this section of the chapter. The list is certainly not exhaustive, not even nearly so, but is merely meant to highlight some key concepts and ideas that successful instructional leaders should know about as they work with teachers to improve teaching (Marzano, 2017). As you read the list, think about ways you might introduce (or reemphasize) these essential teaching concepts or ideas to your faculty.

Above all, as discussed in the introduction and supported by the Instructional Core discussed in Chapter 2, teaching is a process that promotes active student engagement, checking for understanding, and the provision of feedback. If any of these essential three dimensions of teaching are missing, then the teaching act is compromised. This fundamental principle is activated in every lesson. Said more strongly, without incorporating them, teaching has not occurred.

> **SOME RESEARCH-BASED PRACTICES IN TEACHING**
>
> - Allocated, instructional, engaged, and success time are crucial factors in promoting student learning.
> - Wait time increases the amount of time students have to think before responding.
> - Checking for understanding is essential regardless of what subject is taught.
> - Active learning is the most crucial factor for promoting student achievement.
> - Differentiated instruction refers to the varied teaching strategies employed by teachers to address the learning needs of all students.

Best Practice #1: Incorporating Academic Allocated Time, Academic Instructional Time, Academic Engaged Time, and Academic Success Time

Research into teaching effectiveness consistently points to four concepts related to time that are critically important for promoting achievement (Berliner, 1990). Effective principals work with teachers on these four concepts:

1. **Academic Allocated Time** (AAT) is the amount of time teachers assign for various subjects, for example, reading, math, science, etc. Research studies consistently affirm strong relationships between the amount of time allocated by the school administration for a particular subject and achievement. School leaders can investigate and create appropriate AAT by reviewing school policies and schedules with teachers and discussing subject time allocations by grade or department.
2. **Academic Instructional Time** (AIT) refers to the actual amount of time teachers spend in various subjects. Instructional time is influenced by external interruptions (such as excessive announcements over the school loudspeaker and constant interruptions from the main office including monitors coming into class for attendance reports and the like). Minimizing these external interruptions goes far toward increasing the possibility for greater AIT. Classroom-level factors are also significant. For instance, if teachers have difficulty controlling student behavior, AIT will be negatively affected. Therefore, to increase

AIT, schools must minimize classroom interruptions and teachers should have a system of rules and procedures that deal effectively with disciplinary problems and other disruptions. This plan should be implemented with consistency to provide for greater time spent on the allocated curriculum.

3. **Academic Engaged Time** (AET) is the time a student spends attending to academic tasks. Often referred to as "Time on Task," this factor must be present for academic achievement. "Along with the importance of time allocated to instruction by the teacher, the time the students spend 'on task' or engaged in the learning activity, is an important contributor to classroom success" (Stronge, 2007, p. 48). For example, teachers can allocate time for math, and they can spend time instructing their students in the subject, but they will not see results unless the students are on task. According to Ornstein (1990), "Students of teachers who provide more academically engaged time (as well as actual instructional time) learn more than students of teachers who provide relatively less time" (p. 76). Teachers who employ instructional strategies that increase time on task are more effective than those who do not. Research verifies that teachers who engage learners invite all students to actively participate in the lesson, use more positive reinforcement strategies including rewarding on-task behavior, make their lessons appealing, vary the types of questions they pose, distribute their questions to many students, tend to provide step-by-step directions to students, and come to class well prepared.

4. **Academic Success Time** (AST) is the percentage of the academic engaged time during which the student experiences high and medium levels of *successful* learning (Berliner, 1990). This is the most essential factor for promoting academic achievement. Teachers can allocate time, provide instructional time, and ensure on-task behavior, but what does the extant research say about how they can ensure that students are successful? First, a teacher needs to know if students are learning successfully. This can be done by frequently checking for understanding by circulating the room during student independent work and providing situational assistance; calling on nonvolunteers to ascertain attention and comprehension and at times administering a verbal or written quiz. Help can be provided for those students who are experiencing difficulties by using cooperative learning grouping and grouping students who have specific problems in a content area. Utilizing differentiated instruction to meet the needs of all students and provide equal attention to all greatly impacts on student success.

Learning Activity #1

Describe the way you'd introduce and support AAT, AIT, AET, and AST with your faculty.

_____

_____

Best Practice #2: Wait Time

Research on wait time is prolific as it is clear. A simple search on "wait time" will indicate its prolific nature. Research indicates that effective use of wait time is a major factor in promoting student learning. Wait time is an instructional strategy that refers to the amount of time students have to think during questioning. Research indicates that providing between 7 and 10 seconds for students to think before the instructor answers a question or calls on someone else improves student's accurate participation. Teacher-focused instruction decreases and student failure to respond is reduced.

Benefits to wait time include increases in

- the length of student responses;
- student-initiated and appropriate responses;
- the number of students responding;
- student confidence in responding;
- student speculative responses increase;
- student-to-student interactions;
- student evidence to support statements;
- the number of student questions;
- the participation of "slow" students; and
- the variety of student responses.

Successful teachers use wait time in various ways. Here's how one teacher reported his use of wait time: "I pose a question. I don't call on anyone before about 7 seconds even if someone raises a hand immediately. I allow think time. What happens if after 7 seconds no one responds? I ask myself, 'Do I need to rephrase the question?' If so, I do and start again. If not, I ask them to pair and share thoughts about possible answers. I give them about 60–90 seconds. This technique always yields results. Students give their answers. Not always, however, are the answers right, but at least they had time to reflect and respond."

Best Practice #3: Checking for Understanding

The use of formative assessments has received much attention in the literature on classroom effectiveness (Brookhart, 2008; Popham, 2008). Here are a few techniques culled from this literature:

1. Use pair and share: Upon teacher prompt, one student turns to another to repeat or explain the concept just reviewed by the teacher.
2. The Minute Paper (Angelo & Cross, 1993): The teacher takes the last few minutes of class time and asks the students to write down short answers to two questions. The responses can be written on index cards that the teacher hands out or written on the student's own paper. Questions should be open-ended such as: What question(s) do you have about the material covered in today's class? What was the concept that we learned today that was the most difficult for you to understand? List the key concepts from today's class.
3. Reciprocal Teaching: Many forms of this very important teaching strategy can be used (Palincsar & Brown, 1984). Research demonstrates that reciprocal teaching is particularly effective during and after learning content-laden material. One form is as follows:
   1. After having presented relatively difficult material, tell students to close their notebooks and texts and find a partner to "pair and share."
   2. Inform students that one of them should be designated as "Student A" and the other "Student B."
   3. Let Student B tell Student A everything they just learned. Student A cannot ask any questions. Student A records information. As Student B relates the information, Student A pays attention to any errors or omissions.
   4. After about 5 minutes, tell Student A to tell Student B about any errors or omissions. Allow about 3 minutes.
   5. Tell students to now open their notebooks and texts to determine if the information they related to each other is correct.
   6. Teacher checks for understanding.

Best Practice #4: Active Learning

Most students cannot learn unless they are actively engaged with other elements in the Instructional Core. Through extensive classroom observations, researchers have determined that active learning is evident when students are engaging with teachers in active ways (e.g., dialoguing, not merely through recitation wherein the student is left on their own) when students engage with fellow students (e.g., dialoguing with each other, not merely having teachers repeat student responses), and when students are provided opportunities to engage course content (e.g., in its selection). More fundamentally, active learning is fostered when knowledge is viewed as a process of constructing meaning through exploration and when students are provided opportunities to demonstrate their knowledge in different ways.

The research on active learning is extensive. John Dewey (1899) said that people learn best "by doing" (also see Bruner, 1966). Hands-on instructional tasks encourage students to become actively involved in learning. Active learning increases students' interest in the material, makes the material being taught more meaningful, allows students to refine their understanding of the material, and provides opportunities to relate the material to broad contexts.

Active learning reflects constructivist theory. According to constructivist theory, learning is a socially mediated process in which learners construct knowledge in developmentally appropriate ways, and that real learning requires that learners use new knowledge and apply what they have learned (Vygotsky, 1934/1986). These beliefs emphasize "minds-on" learning. This endorses the belief that all learners must be intellectually engaged in the learning process by building on their previous knowledge and experiences and applying their new learning in meaningful contexts. Constructivism also supports the social dimensions of learning; people learn best when actively working with others as partners (e.g., cooperative learning) (Johnson, Johnson, & Johnson-Holubec, 1994). Thus, constructivist pedagogy is aligned with the moral commitment to provide all students with high-quality developmentally appropriate instruction (Udvari-Solner & Kluth, 2007).

More specifically, students who are encouraged to "gather, assemble, observe, construct, compose, manipulate, draw, perform, examine, interview, and collect" are likely to be engaged in meaningful learning opportunities (Davis, 1998, p. 119). Students may, for example, gather facts about 9/11 by exploring primary and secondary sources, even exploring the internet, and then compose essays about key historical figures. Students of diverse learning styles may become involved in cooperative group projects on topics they deem interesting. Students may record their observations about reading selections and react to video segments in personal reaction journals. Students may construct posters demonstrating artifacts, while teams of students may interview survivors and others.

Barak Rosenshine (1971) and others highlighted principles of effective instruction and student engagement that serve to promote student learning and achievement. The most relevant research findings include the following:

- Abstract ideas need to be first made concrete through the use of objects, illustrations, manipulatives, and examples (through hands-on learning).

- Graphic organizers and visual frameworks should be used when introducing new content and when designing student worksheets.
- Inductive (i.e., indirect) instruction is often preferable to deductive (i.e., direct) instruction because the content becomes more meaningful if the learner is guided to independently discover rules, definitions, and attributes.
- Students need to be allowed to interact verbally to process new learning for increased understanding and retention.
- Opportunities for practice must follow instruction.

Finally, in one of the most comprehensive and methodological research studies undertaken, Prince (2004) in an article entitled "Does Active Learning Work? A Review of the Research," concludes that,

> Although the results vary in strength, this study has found support for all forms of active learning examined. . . . The best evidence suggests that faculty should structure their courses to promote collaborative and cooperative environments. . . . Teaching cannot be reduced to formulaic methods and active learning is not the cure for all educational problems. However, there is broad support for the elements of active learning most commonly discussed in the educational literature and analyzed here. (p. 7)[2]

Best Practice #5: Differentiating Instruction

Classrooms are more complex and inclusionary than ever. Teachers must learn how to differentiate instruction to accommodate the learning needs of all students. Effective teachers tend to "recognize individual and group differences among their students and accommodate those differences in their instruction" (Stronge, 2007, p. 57). Differentiated learning takes place when teachers are aware and able to consider and deal with the different learning needs and abilities of their students. Active learning is often utilized within a differentiated learning environment. Here are a few suggestions that might be proffered to teachers:

1. Utilize homogeneous grouping: Identify above-average learners and provide them opportunities to work with students of similar abilities on special activities and projects.
2. Utilize their talents through peer tutoring: Educate and allow these accelerated learners to assist "slower" (different) learners in specific learning activities. Students receiving the assistance will benefit, but so too will the advanced learners. They will benefit emotionally because they are helping fellow students. They learn that all students are unique

and should be valued. They too will learn the material better. I always say that if you want to understand something, teach. These arguments in favor of peer tutoring can be shared with resistant parents who insist that such an activity detracts from the educational experiences of their children.
3. Provide enrichment activities and individualized attention: Do not ignore these accelerated learners by teaching to the "middle." Plan specific lessons for their needs. Plan on meeting and working with them individually.
4. Use cooperative learning: Research indicates that teachers who incorporate cooperative learning strategies promote student achievement.

Learning Activity #2

Describe the way you'd introduce Best Practices #s 2–5:

___

___

Vignette #1: On one of my visits to a high school, I observed a history teacher give a 30-minute lecture on the American Revolution. As the bell rang to begin the class, he stood behind his lectern and spoke nonstop for 30 minutes, occasionally jotting some facts on the board. He then stopped and asked, "Any questions?" After 5 seconds he proceeded to talk for another 15 minutes until the bell rang. As students left the class, they were given a sheet with 15 questions to answer based on the lecture.

I later asked the teacher if this was the usual manner in which he "taught" his classes. He responded, "Of course, Prof. Glanz, after all this is history!"

Learning Activity #3

Describe the way you'd react to this teacher's way of teaching. Is there anything you could think of that we could say to alter his approach to teaching? Why do so many, especially in higher education, overuse lecture? Are their arguments for its prominent use valid? Why or why not? How might you defend more active learning in higher education?

___

___

Extra Bonus: **Three ways of actively engaging students in a lesson**

1. **Reflective Journaling:** A teacher can encourage students to keep reflective journals with guided prompts in which they can document their thoughts, insights, and questions about the lesson content. These journals become an ongoing conversation with the teacher that promotes continuous dialogue and deepens students' understanding of the material as they self-assess their learning progress.
2. **Student-Led Discussions:** Facilitating student-led discussions in the classroom in which students take on the role of moderators, empowers students to actively engage with the material, share perspectives, and explore concepts collaboratively.
3. **Project-Based Learning:** Implementing project-based learning helps students take an active role in designing and executing projects related to the lesson's content. This approach encourages students to delve deeper into the subject matter, apply critical thinking skills, and work together toward meaningful outcomes.

AN OVERVIEW OF BEST PRACTICES IN CURRICULUM

Instructional leadership is about encouraging best practices in the curriculum. To do so requires familiarity with basic concepts involved in curriculum development. Successful instructional leaders facilitate best practices in the curriculum in the following ways, among others:

- Model best practice in the curriculum by reviewing all instructional resources and materials in various content areas.
- Align teaching with curriculum.
- Encourage teachers to review curriculum guidelines and recommend revisions to the instructional program.
- Unpack the standards and convert them into curriculum and instruction.
- Review testing and assessment procedures.
- Invite curriculum specialists from within and outside of the school to help facilitate curriculum revisions and development.

The box below summarizes different ways of approaching or thinking about curriculum development. The list is not exhaustive but is merely meant to highlight some key concepts and ideas that successful instructional leaders should know about as they engage in curricular matters.

SOME RESEARCH-BASED PRACTICES IN CURRICULUM

- **Understand the Curriculum Development Process:** This practice involves "analysis, design, implementation, and evaluation of educational experiences in a school to establish goals, plan experiences, select content, and assess outcomes of school programs" (Wiles & Bondi, 2010, p. 12).
- **Tripod View of Curriculum:** This involves three ways of conceiving curriculum: based on the needs of the learner, the needs of society, or the knowledge base.
- **Two Curriculum Models:** The Tyler rationale involves four steps to consider in developing curriculum. Understanding by Design has become the most popular approach to curriculum design over the past 15 years.
- **Planning, Implementing, and Assessing Teaching and Learning:** This is a practice that involves a three-step curriculum developmental framework.
- **Designing Quality Curriculum:** This involves three guidelines offered by Glatthorn (2000) for designing quality curriculum.

Best Practice #1: Engage Collaboratively in Curriculum Leadership

Curriculum development is a dynamic, interactive, and complex process that serves as the foundation for good teaching practice. Instructional leaders must be actively involved in curriculum leadership. Engaging teachers in helping develop, monitor, and assess curriculum is best practice.

Principals, for instance, play a key role in engaging teachers in discussions about curriculum. They can ask, "What is curriculum?" and "How can we take ownership of what is taught?" In doing so, they encourage teachers to become stakeholders in curriculum development so that they can enrich the educational lives of their students through meaningful and relevant pedagogy. Moreover, effective educators set aside school time for curriculum-based discussions and allow teachers to creatively develop new curricula. The curriculum is not in textbooks, not in worksheets, and not in work devised by administrators. Curriculum development is an ongoing, collaborative process to find new and better ways to match content to students' abilities, interests, and aspirations.

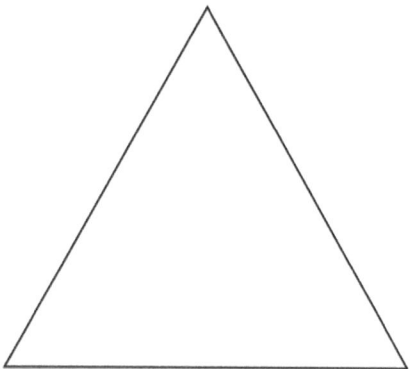

Figure 3.1. The tripod view of curriculum.

Best Practice #2: Understand and Use the Tripod View of Curriculum

A key ingredient to empowering teachers to think about curriculum as an engaging instructional process is to help them explore their beliefs and values of education itself. Principals can ask their teachers, "Where should emphasis be placed when developing curriculum for our students, on knowledge itself, on the learner, or on what society deems most important?"

The "tripod view of curriculum" (Figure 3.1) is important to uncover fundamental beliefs of teachers and others in designing and developing curricula.

Figure 3.1 depicts three emphases or sources in thinking about the curriculum: subject matter (knowledge) considerations, learner's needs, or society's (community's) values. Teachers may be asked to discuss whether "knowledge" or subject matter is most essential. In other words, should instruction be guided by subject matter considerations rather than by societal (communal) or learner needs? Should the needs of learners play the most prominent role in designing a curriculum? Schools, in my view, too often merely pay lip service to meeting student needs. Successful schools, according to research, are ones in which students' learning needs are paramount (Darling-Hammond, 2008).

Best Practice #3: Understand and Apply the Tyler and Understanding by Design Models of Curriculum

In working with teachers to plan for teaching and learning, several curriculum models may serve as guides. One of the most helpful curriculum development models for teachers to easily implement is the one developed by Ralph Tyler (1949). His famous model is practical in the sense that principals can work with teachers to establish curriculum goals that can then be translated into instructional objectives. Through curriculum development, teachers identify learning activities to provide students with meaningful learning experiences.

Widely known as the Tyler rationale, this useful model identifies four steps in curriculum development:

1. What educational purposes should the school seek to attain?
2. What educational experiences can be provided that are likely to attain these purposes?
3. How can these educational experiences be effectively organized?
4. How can we determine whether these purposes are being attained?

Tyler advocated detailed attention to these four questions in developing curriculum. The basic idea to keep in mind about Tyler's model is that four steps are involved whenever curriculum is developed: First, state objectives. According to Tyler, objectives must be stated in behavioral terms so that teachers can assess the extent of student learning. For example, the teacher may state that the "student will be able to identify four of five reasons why the civil war started." Therefore, if the student can only identify two reasons, teachers know that the student has not achieved the objective and needs additional work.

Second, select learning activities. After objectives are articulated, select meaningfully relevant activities to help students accomplish the stated objectives. These learning activities should consider the student's needs and interests. Providing learning activities that motivate students is critical.

Third, organize the learning activities. Learning activities should be concrete and sequential (i.e., one builds on the other). Learning experiences also must be well-integrated according to Tyler. That is, they should relate to each other in a way so that students see rhyme and reason to them and to how they relate to the objectives as well.

Fourth, develop a means of evaluation. Teachers should develop performance measures to determine the extent of student learning. These may take the form of traditional testing (e.g., objectives tests) or alternate forms of assessment, although Tyler focused more on traditional means of evaluation. Tyler's model is predicated on a view of teaching and learning. According to

Tylerian pedagogy, teaching is often conceived as a systematic or organized process in which outcomes are readily discernible, even measurable. His model is a good and practical starting point.

Another more current and prominent curriculum model is Understanding by Design (UbD) (Wiggins & McTighe, 2005). UbD is a backward curricular or unit design model that focuses on the clear identification of the desired learning outcomes before planning the teaching process. It "begins with the end in mind" (Covey, 2004, p. 95) by requiring teachers to identify the big ideas, enduring understandings and essential questions that are found in the unit. After that, the teacher also decides on the skills and knowledge that the student should be able to do and know after the unit. Once all the learning objectives have been identified, the teacher still does not begin to plan the lessons. The next step in the model is to develop assessments by determining what would be considered appropriate evidence of the student's understanding and attainment of the desired results. The teacher uses this information to create both formative and summative assessments, some of which include performance tasks and products. Only then does the teacher begin to plan the lessons and determine what learning experiences and teaching will lead to the predetermined desired results.

This type of unit planning avoids the content-focus design followed by many teachers who just "throw some content and activities" (Wiggins & McTighe, 2005, p. 15) together without a clear sense of the learning objectives. It also eliminates learning activities that are not oriented toward the goals and have no purpose. In content-focus design the lessons are not framed with big ideas and understandings and students are left without a deep understanding of what they are learning because facts remain isolated bits of information that are forgotten as quickly as they are learned. When a teacher uses UbD, a student makes connections between discrete facts, creating a whole picture which then allows them to make sense of and really understand what they have learned. As part of that understanding they are also able to "transfer . . . and to apply the knowledge and skills effectively in realistic tasks and settings" (Wiggins & McTighe, 2005, p. 7).

Best Practice #4: Implement a Curriculum Development Process

Principals can facilitate three key curriculum development steps for teachers that are the same steps used for all lesson planning:

1. Planning for teaching and learning.
2. Implementing the plan.
3. Assessing teaching and learning.

According to Beach and Reinhartz (2000), "These three steps provide a framework for supervisors to use in working with teachers in groups or individually as they develop a blueprint for teaching and learning in classrooms and schools" (p. 199). They outline the three steps of the curriculum development process. The steps are cyclical as the process begins and ends with planning. Units or lessons are modified and improved through this process.

In Step 1, planning for teaching and learning occurs by determining prior knowledge and skills as well as establishing instructional results/proficiencies. In Step 2, the plan is implemented by utilizing varied teaching strategies and activities, monitoring student progress, and providing feedback. During Step 3, teaching and learning are assessed through the use of formative and summative instruments. Modifications are made along the way as well as attention to students who have not mastered the material. Preparation for the next lesson is made. This cyclical process is ongoing for each instructional unit.

Developing curriculum at the planning stage involves determining prior knowledge and skills of learners, establishing instructional outcomes, and reviewing appropriate resources and materials. Teachers and principals plan together at this stage and reflect on the teaching and learning process. During a grade conference, for example, teachers and principals can examine mandated curricula but still be free to develop and match instructional objectives with learner needs and abilities.

Curricular modifications at this stage are possible and indeed recommended to plan for the most meaningful unit of instruction possible. Instructional practices, for instance, in an inclusive classroom will differ dramatically from a more homogenous grouping of students. During this stage, teachers and principals can review the availability of appropriate resources and materials that support instruction. They can also address possible teaching strategies and activities, goals and objectives, assessment procedures (always keeping the end in mind), content or subject matter, and standards that must be met. Principals play a key role in this opening step of the curriculum development process as they challenge and lead teachers to consider the following:

- Content matched to the developmental level of students
- Prerequisite knowledge and skills before undertaking a new unit of instruction
- Inductive and deductive teaching approaches
- Selection and appropriateness of learning experiences
- Sequencing of learning experiences
- Selection and appropriateness of assessment instruments

Beach and Reinhartz (2000) remind us that "the success of the curriculum depends on the quality of planning and the decisions that teachers make as they prepare for instruction" (p. 201).

During the second step of the curriculum development process plans are implemented. Teaching is the process of implementing curricular plans. Curriculum and teaching are conceived as very much interrelated. During this step, teachers present their lessons using appropriate and varied strategies and activities. Teachers also model skills and monitor student progress (see Figure 2.2).

The third step of assessing teaching and learning is critically important. If students are not learning, the curriculum development process requires modifications. Perhaps instructional objectives need reconsideration, teaching strategies may need revision, or reteaching and review may be necessary. Leaders can also assist teachers by engaging them in informal and formal conversations about units of instruction. They can assist teachers in gathering learning data from a variety of sources beyond the traditional pencil and paper test. Alternative forms of assessment are shared with teachers that may include, among others, student portfolios that include work samples and journal writing.

It is critical to note that even if teachers are mandated to implement state or ministry-derived curricula, teachers can still create exciting and innovative lessons geared to student's needs, interests, and abilities. The next best practice deals with ways in which teachers can even modify state curricula and prepackaged programs.

Best Practice #5: Understand How to Design Quality Curriculum

Glatthorn (2000, pp. 11–12) highlights several guidelines for developing quality curriculum, some of which are reviewed here:

1. Structure the curriculum to allow for greater depth and less superficial coverage. Teachers should engage students in meaningful and detailed lessons that involve problem-solving projects and activities and critical thinking teaching strategies. Such activities and strategies form the basis for any topic to be covered during the course of the school year. Rather than rushing to "cover" topics or "teaching for the test," teachers should give students problem-solving and critical thinking skills that they, on their own, can apply to any topic.
2. Structure and deliver the curriculum so that it facilitates the mastery of essential skills and knowledge of the subjects. Providing students

with a rich and deep knowledge base is primary but should be incorporated with problem-solving strategies that are realistic and meaningful to students.
3. Structure the curriculum so that it is closely coordinated. Coordinating content within lessons and among units over the course of the school year is imperative so that curriculum is sequential and well-organized.
4. Emphasize both the academic and the practical. Relating content to students' lived experiences is important to increase student learning. Hands-on activities, when feasible, are very much warranted.

In sum, curriculum involves an analysis of all the learning experiences that occur in school. Effective instructional leaders involve teachers in curriculum development. Prepackaged curricula, or curricula designed by outside consultants with minimal involvement of school personnel, is not best practice. If teachers are involved in the curriculum process, they assume ownership and are more likely to implement said revisions. Even an exceptionally designed curriculum created by someone else may be less likely used because of the lack of teacher involvement and ownership.

Curriculum involvement, however, requires requisite curriculum knowledge and skills. Effective principals draw upon the skills of curriculum supervisors and consultants who share their knowledge and experience with faculty. Good teaching does not occur in isolation of curriculum. Effective principals as instructional leaders know this fact.

Effective principals are involved in these curricular activities, among others:

- Reviewing state curriculum guidelines and procedures.
- Organizing curriculum discussion groups at faculty and grade conferences with teachers.
- Assigning curriculum facilitators among the faculty and assistant principals.
- Reviewing instructional materials and resources.
- Evaluating the relevancy of curriculum materials and resources.
- Involving, most importantly, teachers in the curriculum design and revision process.
- Soliciting input from others in the curriculum process (e.g., curriculum specialists, parents, and students).
- Examining the relationship between teaching and curriculum.
- Assessing the impact of curriculum materials on student achievement.
- Engaging teachers continually in discussion of teaching, learning, and curriculum.

Learning Activity #4

Describe the way you, as a school leader, could implement the ideas to better take control over the curriculum:

_____

_____

Vignette #2: One principal told me, quite bluntly, "We are very busy. Thankfully, we don't need to think too much about the curriculum. After all, we have the mandated curricula in most subjects. My job is to ensure that teachers keep up to that curriculum."

Learning Activity #5

There are advantages and disadvantages to prepackaged, state- (or otherwise) imposed curricula. Discuss. Is there a way to still utilize the curricular strategies discussed in this chapter and still adhere to mandated curricular guidelines and requirements?

_____

_____

An Overview of Best Practices in Professional Development

Professional development (PD) is among the most powerful ways to enhance and improve the knowledge and skills of educators (Popova et al., 2021). Unfortunately, the way in which PD is introduced and practiced is flawed.

The first flawed assumption is that a certified teacher needs little continued preparation to do their job. Every craft or profession needs a sustained program to help workers do a better job. Technologies advance, new theories emerge, and new skills are needed to handle the ever-changing challenges in 21st-century schooling. Put simply, everyone can continue to learn and grow professionally, and a thoughtful and effective PD program is a necessity, not merely an option.

Parenthetically, a word about the term "training" that is too often employed in the education literature. We "train" animals; we don't train human beings. The word "train" comes out of behavioristic psychology that smacks of a Pavlovian type of conditioning or manipulation that aims to control, reprogram, and redesign someone. Rather, one should use words such as "prepare," "professionally develop or improve," and so forth.

The discussion in this section is rather straightforward. It describes a fundamental approach to PD that all schools should adopt.

> **SOME RESEARCH-BASED PRACTICES IN PROFESSIONAL DEVELOPMENT**
>
> Professional development is a process of supporting teacher's work and student learning through systematic, continuous, meaningful, knowledge-based workshops and seminars around collaboratively developed topics.

BEST PRACTICES: COLLABORATIVELY PLANNING AND IMPLEMENTING SUSTAINABLE AND MEANINGFUL PROFESSIONAL DEVELOPMENT

By providing PD experiences (i.e., workshops/seminars/courses), principals provide opportunities for teachers to engage in instructional conversations about relevant issues affecting teaching and learning. PD may include, among others, sessions on teaching strategies, studying the latest theory and research on practice, receiving feedback on teaching, providing resources for practice, coaching (peer or otherwise), etc.

The literature on PD is vast (Reeves, 2010). Almost all schools provide some sort of PD learning opportunities for teachers. Although PD sessions have been offered, many individuals criticize the manner in which PD is planned and delivered. Potentially, PD is undoubtedly an invaluable learning program to support teachers and improve student learning. However, much of professional (sometimes referred to as "staff") development is content weak, episodic, and at its worst, irrelevant to the needs of teachers.

Principals, as instructional leaders, realize that PD, well-conceived, planned, and assessed, is vital to improving teaching and student learning. Best practice in PD points to several components as necessary (Lieberman, 1995):

- *Purposeful and articulated:* Goals for a PD program must be developed, examined, critiqued, and assessed for relevance. These goals must be stated in some formal way so that all educators concerned with the PD program are clear about its intent and purpose.
- *Participatory and collaborative:* Too often PD is top-driven, even at times by administrative fiat. Such programs are less effective because

teachers, for whom PD serves the greatest benefit, are not actively involved in its design, implementation, and assessment. Best practice in PD requires wide participation by all stakeholders.
- *Knowledge-based and discipline-based:* PD must be based on the most relevant and current research in the field. Also, teachers will not value PD unless it contains, in the words of one teacher, "some substance, . . . something I can take back to the classroom." Moreover, PD should be, at times, targeted by discipline. Often, high school English teachers may want and need a workshop on a topic or approach quite different from, say, biology teachers.
- *Focused on student learning:* According to Lindsrum and Speck (2004), "Educators must never forget that the objective of professional development is to increase student learning" (p. 156). Principals and committees that are responsible for planning PD programs should consider first and foremost the teacher behaviors or activities that most directly impact student learning and then "work backward to pinpoint the knowledge, skills, and attitudes educators must have" (p. 157).
- *Ongoing:* Too much PD is of the one-shot variety. A leader delivers a workshop, for instance, then leaves without any follow-up. Such efforts have marginal value at best. PD opportunities must be made available continuously so that ideas and practices are sustained. PD cannot impact classroom practice in a significant way unless workshops and programs are continually offered.
- *Developmental:* PD must not only be ongoing but developmental, that is, building gradually on teacher knowledge and skills in a given area or topic.
- *Analytical and reflective:* PD opportunities must promote instructional dialogue and thinking about teaching practice and purposefully address ways of helping students achieve more. Also, PD must be continuously assessed in terms of its relevance and value to teachers.

The latest research findings indicate that PD to have significant effects on student achievement requires at least dozens of hours on a given topic (Brandefur et al., 2016; Gore et al., 2021).

Providing instructional leadership by focusing on best practices in PD is an important responsibility of the principal (Kilag & Sasan, 2023). Unfortunately, much of what currently takes place as PD is not very useful for teachers (Bean, 2021). Supervisors can contribute greatly to PD by engaging in these leadership behaviors:

- In word and deed, place emphasis on improving teaching and promoting learning.

- Involve teachers in planning, implementing, and assessing PD.
- Utilize experts in PD as consultants.
- Provide options or alternatives to traditional practices of PD.
- Draw links between PD and student achievement.

Learning Activity #6

Describe your experiences with PD and the way schools/districts could better plan and produce meaningful PD. Explain the manner in which you would establish and run a PD in your school.

_____
_____

Vignette #3: After visiting a school over a two-day period, I concluded that PD as best practice was absent in this school. At our exit meeting, I mentioned to the school's leadership team that I noticed after perusing the school's overall and instructional budget that PD had no budget line. The principal retorted, "Why, of course, it's there." He took the budget I was holding, gazed at it for a second, and then pointed, "There it is!" I looked. He had pointed to "Misc."

Learning Activity #7

What message can we infer from the principal's response? What might we say to any school leader to place greater prominence on PD?

_____
_____

OVERVIEW OF BEST PRACTICES IN SUPERVISION

Supervision is a process that engages teachers in instructional dialogue to improve teaching and promote student achievement. Principals should view themselves, and be seen, as "teachers of teachers." This notion is predicated on the condition that principals have adequate teaching experience themselves and possess the knowledge and skills to communicate good teaching practice to teachers. Principals, as instructional leaders, understand how to work with teachers to improve teaching and promote student learning. Principals should implement a variety of instructional improvement strategies, as explained here.

Parenthetically, traditional supervision, often referred to by teachers as "the dog and pony show" wherein teachers are notified in advance of an observation, then prepare their "best" lesson for a supervisor to observe, followed by a written supervisory letter that highlights good teaching practices and areas needed for improvement. These formal observations do not seriously encourage instructional dialogue and reflection.

At the other end of the spectrum, short "walk-through" visits that offer little in-depth understanding of teaching practices are similarly unproductive.[3] That is not to say that visiting classrooms is unwarranted. Supervisors must demonstrate their commitment to teaching excellence by visiting classrooms often and being available to teachers as resources. However, in terms of making a significant improvement in teaching and learning, they have no impact.

Vignette #4: I asked my students to explain the meaning of "supervision" after a recent course I taught. I also asked them to compare the nature of supervision described in my course to their previous experiences and understandings. Here is a representative response from a student in that class:

> *Educational supervision is a collaborative dynamic, and continuous instructional process, not aimed at changing behavior, but rather encouraging nonjudgmental discussion and reflection about teaching.*
>
> *Prior to this course, supervision, for me as a principal, was a yearly event in which I would enter a classroom, sometimes with advance notice, to observe a lesson while sitting in the back of the room. On occasion, I would make a passing comment about how much I enjoyed the lesson. On other occasions, I would engage the teacher afterward, usually in my office, and provide feedback on her effective teaching practices. I'd almost always give her suggestions for improvement. We usually had a discussion of no more than three minutes. In the end, I had no idea if the teacher followed up on my suggestions. For me and the teacher the supervision process was completed.*

SOME RESEARCH-BASED PRACTICES IN SUPERVISION

One Size Does Not Fit All (including **PCOWBIRDS**): Differentiating supervisory approaches is recommended. Given teachers' levels of experience and expertise, establish a variety of supervisory options for teachers to improve and grow professionally.

Best Practice: Establish a Differentiated Approach to Supervision

Some of the best approaches to supervision that go way beyond "the dog and pony show," and can encourage deep reflection and discussion about teaching practices are listed here (two of the most practical books on these strategies are Glickman et al., [2017] and Sullivan and Glanz [2013]):

a. Clinical Supervisory Model: With the assistance of a consultant the administration should start to incorporate a clinical supervision (preconference, short observations, and a postconference) process that encourages deep reflection about teaching practices. With this model, supervisors, do not "tell" teachers what is "right" or "wrong" but rather offer data through the use of observation forms or instruments to teachers and then begin an instructional conversation with teachers encouraging them to reflect on their practices in the classroom (Sullivan & Glanz, 2013). Only teachers themselves can change their teaching practices. Supervisors may facilitate but cannot and should not mandate change.
b. Demo Lessons and Videotaping: Faculty or department meetings should include, at times, analyses of videotaped (or recorded) teaching episodes. A supervisor can first volunteer to have themself videotaped for 10 minutes, to be then used for viewing and discussion by a group of teachers. Such practices build trust and a learning community in a school (DuFour et al., 2009).
c. Intervisitations: Most teachers rarely have seen a colleague teach. Providing release time for colleagues to observe each other and then providing time for discussion is recommended. Their experiences can later be shared at a department or whole faculty meeting.
d. Peer Coaching: A pair of teachers alternate periods observing each other and use data to engage in conversations. Peer coaching may differ from the strategy above in the sense that such observations are long term.
e. Action Research: Encouraging teachers, instead of the "dog-pony" observation requirement (this is useful for tenured, experienced teachers), to engage in a project in which they identify (on their own or with a colleague) a problem they are experiencing in the classroom, compose some research questions, gather data to answer them, reflect on findings, take actions, etc. is an invaluable supervisory asset (Bambrick-Santoyo, 2010).
f. Book Studies: Teachers or administrators can distribute copies of a book (on pedagogy, or in a particular discipline) and then engage, in meetings, in conversations about strategies learned for classroom implementation.

g. Reflective Journaling: Again, an alternative to traditional supervision might be to offer teachers' choices to record journal reflections of their teaching over time to then be shared, in discussion, with another colleague, or presented at a faculty meeting, etc.
h. Lesson Studies: Teachers collaboratively plan a lesson (perhaps in association with the curriculum mapping process), each presents the lesson to a class, and then meet together to discuss successes, questions, and challenges (Perry & Lewis, 2009).
i. Instructional Rounds: A small group of teachers and others visit a classroom of a colleague. The visit may last 15 or so minutes. The focus is on the instructional core, not on the competence of the teacher. The discussion that ensues should never be judgmental. Rather, focus is on describing anecdotally the varied classroom interactions. There are various models used for such rounds (see approaches, for instance, Marzano & Brown, 2009, especially at http://www.marzanoresearch.com/documents/Marzano_Protocol.pdf).
j. Professional Growth Plans: Individual teachers should have access to these plans as well. Utilize the talents of experienced teachers by encouraging them and drawing on their years in the classroom to help mentor less experienced teachers or conduct workshops for each other. In many cases, it is not necessary to call upon consultants from outside the school to offer PD; utilize the talent and expertise that exists in a school. Supervisors, during the process, meet with teachers annually to establish new instructional goals that they would like to focus on for the year, such as incorporating technology into their teaching. Assessment and revision of goals are made at the end of each year via a collaborative discussion between supervisor and teacher, or even among teachers as a team.

Aside from these supervisory strategies that have the potential to encourage conversation about good teaching practices, here are some other suggestions to enhance a supervisory program known as PCOWBIRDS:

- Plans: Planning is integral to instructional success and the principal as an educational leader should help a teacher develop appropriate and meaningful instructional activities and learning experiences. Checking plans, offering suggestions, coplanning, reviewing procedures, and framing thought-provoking questions, among other important aspects, are essential. Supervision, then, involves assisting teachers to better plan their lessons and units of instruction. Avoid simple checking of plans. Rather, engage teachers in deep conversations about various aspects of the planning and revision processes.

- Conferences: Conferencing with teachers, formally and informally, to share ideas and develop alternate instructional strategies is an essential supervisory responsibility. Meeting and talking with teachers throughout the day and school year on instructional matters are essential. The focus as an instructional leader must be on teaching and learning. Sharing insights, reviewing recent research, and engaging in reflective practice are very important. Formal and informal conferencing must be continuous and should involve teachers in the planning and agenda of conferences. The key to establishing a school culture that fosters instructional dialogue to improve teaching and learning is to consider such activity the number one priority and, thus, devote time and energy to ensuring and nurturing it. A supervisor who truly believes in instructional quality will find the time to do this vital work.
- Observations: An educational leader should offer their expertise by both formally and informally observing classroom interactions. A skilled principal who utilizes various observation systems can facilitate instructional improvement by documenting classroom interaction so that a teacher might reflect upon and react to what has been observed. Providing teachers with evidence of classroom interaction is fundamental to begin helping them understand what they are doing or not doing to promote student learning. Observations play a key role in supervision.
- Bulletins: Bulletins, journals, reports, and newsletters can be disseminated to interested faculty. One of my teachers became interested in cooperative learning after attending a reading conference. I sustained her interest by placing several articles about cooperative learning in her mailbox. Principals should be conversant with the literature of various fields and subscribe to various journals including *Educational Leadership*, *Kappan*, *Elementary School Journal*, *Instructor*, *Teaching K–12*, *Journal of Learning Disabilities*, etc. Principals should always be on the alert for relevant articles, bulletins, and publications that encourage and support instructional improvement (see Appendix I for much more).
- Resources: Principals should make available for teachers a variety of instructional materials and technologies to enhance instructional improvement. Using textbooks, trade books, computers, and other relevant technological resources are important to support an instructional program.
- Demonstration Lessons: A principal presumably is a teacher-of-teachers. A principal is not necessarily the foremost teacher in a school, but they should feel comfortable in providing "demo" lessons for teachers, when appropriate. Providing such lessons enhances supervisory credibility among teachers and provides instructional support.

Parenthetically, I once noticed during a formal observation, that the teacher was not using wait time effectively. He posed good questions but waited only about 2 seconds before calling on someone. I suggested that he watch me teach a lesson and notice how long I wait after posing a question before calling on a pupil. These observations were the basis for a follow-up conference at which we discussed the research on "wait time" and the advantages of waiting before calling on a pupil. As the saying goes, "A picture is worth a thousand words." Having this particular teacher watch me demonstrate effective use of "wait time" was more valuable than had I merely told him what to do. Competent supervisors not only "suggest" how to do something, but they also must "demonstrate" how it should be done.

Learning Activity #8

What would it take for a school leader to implement these alternative strategies to traditional supervision?

___

___

Extra Bonus #1: One More Alternative to Traditional Supervision

Portfolios for Differentiated Instruction is an approach to supervision that involves teachers creating portfolios of their work to demonstrate their expertise in a particular area of teaching. In this approach, teachers select an area of expertise and create a portfolio of their work in that area, which is then reviewed by an administrator or teacher leader (colleague) who provides feedback and suggestions for improvement. It can promote their growth in teaching by providing them with opportunities to reflect on their own teaching practices, identify areas of their teaching that need improvement, and develop strategies for addressing those areas.

Extra Bonus #2: Supervision Should Be Differentiated

What follows are different approaches that a supervisor can take to provide feedback to teachers. Different teachers need different approaches depending on level of experience, personality, and other factors. Moreover, varying school circumstances call for a range of approaches. For teachers to learn and grow they need to be involved to some degree in constructing their own knowledge.

1. In **Directive Informational Feedback** the coach, supervisor, or mentor takes a more authoritative/directive role. They provide clear instructions, guidance, and specific suggestions for improvement to the new or fairly new teacher. This type of feedback is more one-sided, with the supervisor providing specific feedback and directions to help the neophyte develop skills or achieve certain goals.
2. The **Collaborative Approach** involves a shared dialogue between the supervisor/mentor and teacher who has several years of teaching experience. They engage in reflective discussions, jointly exploring instructional practices and seeking solutions together. This differentiated approach emphasizes mutual learning and growth. They both discuss the teacher's performance, strengths, and areas for improvement. The observer encourages open dialogue, listening, and exchange of ideas. The teacher is encouraged to self-assess and provide suggestions and insights. Together, they collaboratively design goals and action plans for improvement.
3. With **Self-Directed Feedback** the experienced teacher takes the leading role in discussing teaching through self-assessment, reflecting on their own performance, and identifying areas for improvement or enrichment. The facilitator-colleague acts more as a reflective mirror, helping to clarify any instructional issues. The teacher is the one calling the shots, the supervisor is more of an enabler who provides the framework to allow the discussion and change to occur.

OVERVIEW OF BEST PRACTICES IN EVALUATION

The views presented in this final section of the chapter are controversial. Based on my years of research and experience with many evaluation systems, I have come to these conclusions:

- There are no evaluation systems or approaches that fundamentally improve teaching. Whether it's the use of a school-developed evaluation form or a state imposed evaluative instrument, teachers do not improve their teaching after having been evaluated.

  In fact, among today's most respected authorities in teacher evaluation, Helen Hazi (2022a) acknowledges this. She describes the state of teacher evaluation as "dysfunctional" (p. 199). She cites James Popham, a well-known authority on teacher evaluation and educational assessment when he states, "The evaluation of America's schoolteachers is with few exceptions, an anemic and impotent enterprise—promising much but producing little" (p. 199). Her work over the years reveals

examples of such dysfunction on many levels (Hazi, 2016). More recently, she has even charged that an alternative to traditional evaluation is imperative (Hazi, 2022). Most recently, she advocated a form of self-evaluation to replace traditional approaches to teacher evaluation (Hazi, 2021).
- Supervision, not evaluation, is viewed by most experts as the center for the improvement of instruction (Zepeda & Ponticell, 2019). If a school has an excellent supervisory system in place, then there is no need for evaluating teachers, except in two specific cases or situations involving accountability:
  1. To ensure a beginning teacher's competence, especially before receiving tenure, a teacher should be formally evaluated to ensure minimal teaching competency. For such a purpose, the selection of a fair and suitable evaluative instrument or system is required. The literature is replete with lists of such evaluative measurements. School leaders and district officials have the moral imperative to ensure that whatever system is employed is fair and matches the requirements of the position and expectations of school officials. Moreover, more than one measure must be taken with ample support for the new teacher to remediate any possible deficiencies. Only after a thorough process should a judgment be made. In this case, evaluation is indeed important but only as an accountability function, that is, to ensure the basic competence of the teacher.
  2. A second possible use of a teacher evaluation instrument (local or state created) is to, as objectively as possible, evaluate a tenured teacher, should the situation arise that complaints are leveled against them, although originally good, has, for a variety of possible reasons, experienced burnout. Here too a fair and unbiased evaluative process must be employed.

Aside from these two exceptional cases, if a school has a vibrant supervisory program as explained above under Best Practices in Supervision, then teacher evaluation, as such, is no longer necessary. In sum, evaluation is employed to ensure teaching competency. It does not foster improvement. Supervision is the process that schools should employ to assist teachers to grow professionally in terms of teaching ability. Continued PD plays a significant role in this effort.

So, what's the best practice for teacher evaluation advocated here? Eliminate it, except in the two aforementioned situations. Otherwise, build a vibrant supervisory system that encourages nonjudgmental, supportive, ongoing, and deep conversations about teaching utilizing a variety of approaches as explained above.[4]

Learning Activity #9
Describe and share with colleagues your reaction to the discussion above.

_____

_____

CONCLUSION

This chapter highlighted several basic topics aimed to strengthen a school's instructional program. The chapter was not meant to be exhaustive. Still, the teaching skills and approaches that were discussed are fundamental to fostering better teaching in the classroom. The curricular suggestions were aimed to better align teaching with the objectives of the curriculum. The nature of PD should conform to the needs of teachers, and teacher evaluation should be utilized in certain exceptional cases with much of the instructional emphasis placed on supervision.

In the next chapter, a case study is presented to illustrate a school's beginning attempts and steps to transform and improve the instructional program. The conclusion here, most fundamentally, is framed around a school leader's primary responsibility, which is to improve teaching and promote student learning. Through such an instructional effort, students may best be able to achieve their learning potential.

REFERENCES

Angelo, T. A., & Cross, K. P. (1993). *Classroom assessment techniques.* Jossey-Bass.
Bambrick-Santoyo, P. (2010). *Driven by data: A practical guide to improving instruction.* Jossey-Bass.
Beach, D. M., & Reinhartz, J. (2000). *Supervisory leadership: Focus on instruction.* Allyn and Bacon.
Bean, S. (2021, February 26). 5 common complaints about professional development from educators. LinkedIn. https://www.linkedin.com/pulse/5-common-complaints-professional-development-from-educators-bean/
Berliner, D. C. (1990). What's all the fuss about instructional time? In M. Ben-Peretz & R. Bromm (Eds.), *The nature of time in schools: Theoretical concepts and perceptions.* Teachers College Press.
Brandefur, J. I., Thiede, K., Strother, S., Jesse, D., & Sutton, J. (2016). The effects of professional development on mathematics achievement. *Journal of Curriculum & Teaching.* http://dx.doi.org/10.5430/jct.v5n2p95
Brookhart, S. M. (2008). *How to give effective feedback to your students.* Association for Supervision and Curriculum Development.

Bruner, J. S. (1966). *Toward a theory of instruction.* Belknap Press.
Covey, S. R. (2004). *The 7 habits of highly effective people.* Simon and Schuster.
Darling-Hammond, L. (2008). Teacher learning that supports student learning. In B. Z. Presseisen (Ed.), *Teaching for intelligence* (2nd ed.). Corwin.
David, J. L. (2007). What research says about classroom walk-throughs. *Educational Leadership,* 65(4), 81–82. https://www.ascd.org/el/articles/classroom-walk-throughs
Davis, Jr., O. L. (1998). Beyond beginnings: From "hands-on" to "minds-on." *Journal of Curriculum and Supervision, 13,* 119–122.
Dewey, J. (1899). *The school and society.* The University of Chicago Press.
DuFour, R., DuFour, R., & Eaker, R. (2009). *Revisiting professional learning communities at work: New insights for improving schools.* Solution Tree.
Glatthorn, A. A. (2000). *Developing a quality curriculum.* Association for Supervision and Curriculum Development.
Glickman, C. D., Gordon, S. P., & Ross-Gordon, J. (2017). *SuperVision and instructional leadership: A developmental approach.* Pearson.
Gore, J. M., Miller, A., Fray, L., Harris, J., & Prieto, E. (2021). Improving student achievement through professional development: Results from a randomized controlled trial of Quality Teaching Rounds. *Teaching and Teacher Education, 101.* https://doi.org/10.1016/j.tate.2021.103297
Hazi, H. M. (2016). *Educators challenging teacher evaluation in a high stakes climate in the states.* Paper presented at the annual conference of the American Educational Research Association, Washington, DC.
Hazi, H. M. (2019). Coming to understand the wicked problem of teacher evaluation. In S. J. Zepeda & J. Ponticell (Eds.), *Handbook of educational supervision* (pp. 183–207). Wiley-Blackwell.
Hazi, H. M. (2021). A swerve in times of crises: Rethinking teacher evaluation anew. In J. Glanz (Ed.), *Crisis and pandemic leadership: Implications for meeting the needs of students, teachers, and parents* (pp. 47–58). Rowman & Littlefield.
Hazi, H. M. (2022). Reconsidering the dual purposes of teacher evaluation. *Teachers and Teaching, 28*(7), 811–825. https://doi.org/10.1080/13540602.2022.2103533
Johnson, D. W., Johnson, R. T., & Johnson-Holubec, E. (1994). *Cooperative learning in the classroom.* Association for Supervision and Curriculum Development.
Kilag, O. K. T., & Sasan, J. M. (2023). Unpacking the role of instructional leadership in teacher professional development. *Advanced Qualitative Research, 1*(1). https://doi.org/10.31098/xxx
Lieberman, A. (1995). *The work of restructuring schools: Building from the ground up.* Teachers College Press.
Lindsrom, P. H., & Speck, M. (2004). *The principal as professional development leader.* Corwin.
Marzano, R. J. (2017). *The new art and science of teaching.* Association of Supervision and Curriculum Development.
Marzano, R. J., & Brown, J. L. (2009). *The handbook for the art and science of teaching.* Association for Supervision and Curriculum Development.

Ornstein, A. C. (1990). *Institutionalized learning in America.* Transaction Publishers.

Palincsar, A. S., & Brown, A. L. (1984). Reciprocal teaching of comprehension-fostering and comprehension-monitoring activities. *Cognition and Instruction, 1*(2), 117–175. https://doi.org/10.1207/s1532690xci0102_1

Perry, R. R., & Lewis, C. C. (2009). What is successful adaptation of lesson study in the US? *Journal of Educational Change, 10,* 365–391. https://doi.org/10.1007/s10833-008-9069-7

Popham, W. J. (2008). *Classroom assessment: What teachers need to know* (5th ed.). Allyn and Bacon.

Popova, A., Evans, D. K., Breeding, M. E., & Arancibia, V. (2021). Teacher professional development around the world: The gap between evidence and practice. *The World Bank Research Observer, 37*(1), 107–136. https://doi.org/10.1093/wbro/lkab006.

Prince, M. (2004). Does active learning work: A review of the research. *Journal of Engineering Education, 93*(3), 223–231. https://doi.org/10.1002/j.2168-9830.2004.tb00809.x.

Reeves, D. B. (2010). *Transforming professional development into student results.* Association for Supervision and Curriculum Development.

Rosenshine, B. (1971). *Teaching behaviors and student achievement.* National Federation for Educational Research.

Shaked, H. (2018). Why principals often give overly high ratings on teacher evaluations. *Studies in Educational Evaluation, 59,* 150–157. https://haimshaked.com/wp-content/uploads/2019/07/pdf-16.pdf

Stronge, J. H. (2007). *Qualities of effective teaching* (2nd ed.). Association for Supervision and Curriculum Development.

Sullivan, S. (2006). Monitoring under the guise of reflective practice. *Supervision and Instructional Leadership AERA SIG Newsletter,* pp. 2–3.

Sullivan, S., & Glanz, J. (2013). *Supervision that improves teaching: Strategies and techniques* (4th ed.). Corwin.

Tyler, R. W. (1949). *Basic principles of curriculum and instruction.* The University of Chicago Press.

Udvari-Solner, A., & Kluth, P. (2007). *Joyful learning: Active and collaborative learning in inclusive classrooms.* Corwin.

Vygotsky, L. (1934/1986). *Thought and language.* The MIT Press.

Wiggins, G., & McTighe, J. (2005). *Understanding by design* (2nd ed.). Association for Supervision and Curriculum Development.

Wiles, J. W., & Bondi, J. (2010). *Curriculum development: A guide to practice* (8th ed.). Prentice Hall.

Zepeda, S. J., & Ponticell, J. A. (Eds.). *The Wiley handbook of educational supervision.* Wiley Blackwell.

NOTES

1. At the outset of this chapter that aims to convey practical strategies, it should be stated that we should have some hesitancy with any approach, in general, which is somewhat technical and positivistic. This means that one should not conclude that if a teacher or school leader incorporates every idea in this chapter that it will automatically lead to improved student achievement. Education and teaching, in particular, are complex and contextual, and are affected by many factors, sometimes beyond one's control (Fischer et al., 2020). Still, these research-based, and common-sense ideas can go a long way toward improving instructional quality in schools.

2. The role of artificial intelligence at the time of this writing is transforming our world. Although its impact is still in its incipient stage, its use in education as a tool to enhance student engagement and active learning has much promise.

3. Jane David (2007), in reviewing extant research, explains that walk-throughs, "also called learning walks, quick visits, and data walks," are "touted as a systematic way to gather helpful data on instructional practices" (p. 81). In explaining the idea behind the concept, she says principals, for example, might "want to know whether teachers are able to put into practice their recent training on quick-writes and pair-shares" (p. 81). David, reviewing the little research available on walk-throughs, explains that according to one study, "administrators find walk-throughs more useful than do teachers (who rarely receive individual feedback)" (p. 81). David points out "significant risks" with such practices. She says when a climate of trust and improvement is not secured in a school, then walk-throughs are perceived "as compliance checks, increasing distrust and tension" (p. 82). David, in her article, seems to suggest, however, that walk-throughs if appropriately implemented can play "a constructive role" in instructional improvement (p. 82). She advocates proper preparation for observers, adequate communication of the purposes of walk-throughs, and recommends that it not merely be used to monitor implementation of some school-wide practice.

When employed in most settings I visited, they were viewed as inspectional because they resembled check-list approaches to supervision of the past. Short cuts and quick fixes, expedient and efficient as they are, are not conducive to classroom and school improvement. In support of such a view, Sullivan (2006) explains that walk-throughs "shed light on an approach to classroom observation that can become monitoring couched in the language of teacher growth and reflective practice" (p. 2).

4. Perhaps the most recent devastating research report that, I believe, supports my position about abolishing teacher evaluation, in most cases, comes from the work of Shaked (2018). He points to four almost intractable features of teacher evaluation: its practice is perceived as low value with high time investment; its ineffectiveness to improve teaching; its imprecision in measuring teaching effectiveness; and its impingement on interpersonal relationships between teachers and administrators.

Chapter 4

Learning to Lead Instructional Change by Transforming School Culture to Support and Improve Teaching and Learning for All

This chapter will highlight some of the literature on school change and present concrete suggestions for implanting the changes needed to achieve high-quality instruction. A case study and follow-up discussion will be presented demonstrating some of the efforts of one high school that attempted to transform its instructional program.

FOCUS QUESTIONS

1. How does one go about changing a school's culture that currently relies on traditional methods of teaching, curriculum, professional development (PD), supervision, and evaluation?
2. What theory or theories of change would you apply if you wanted to improve your school's instructional program?
3. How does one practically go about starting to change traditional instructional practices?
4. Have you ever been part of an instructional transformation of any sort in your school experience? Describe.
5. What suggestions could you offer to go about transforming a school's culture that focuses on best practices as described in the previous chapter?

INSTRUCTIONAL TRANSFORMATION IN THE LITERATURE

Much of the recent literature on school change emerged from the work of Michael Fullan's (2008) "key drivers for change" in his discussion of "change knowledge." His work, it should be noted, is rooted in the groundbreaking work done decades earlier by Seymour Sarason (1982) in his book entitled *The Culture of the School and the Problem of Change*. Sarason posited that change occurs most fundamentally by addressing a school's culture, that is, the beliefs and actions of stakeholders about teaching and learning. Otherwise, change is ephemeral and ineffective.

Change is inevitable as Fullan, Sarason, and others argue because of the ever-increasing complexity of a school's diverse environment. Educators in the 21st century confront a plethora of challenges. For example, there are more students than ever identified with emotional and learning issues (because our diagnostic tools and awareness have improved); communal pressures that compel school leaders to remain responsive to a growing, varied, and diverse constituency is ever-present; technological innovations (especially with the advent of artificial intelligence) affect the nature of learning and teaching; the political and social landscape has been affected, more than ever in recent times, by polarized vested interests, etc. These internal and external vicissitudes inevitably challenge school leaders' convictions and intestinal fortitude. Because problems are more intractable today, educators have relied on a theory of leadership to guide their work in schools. Transformational school leadership theory provides foundational guidance for school leaders, as described in Chapter 1.

Related to the theme of *Creating a Culture of Excellence*, a transformational visionary agenda includes a redesign or, at the very least, a reexamination of a school's commitment to teacher quality, teacher growth, instructional excellence, and student learning. Although no theory of leadership is without criticism, transformational leadership informs the work of school leaders. These leaders who want to transform the culture of their schools, champion a vision of instructional excellence that includes:

1. Best practices in teaching (with attention to the "Instructional Core," as outlined in Chapter 2)
2. Best practices in curriculum
3. Best practices in professional development and supervision both of which were addressed in Chapter 3

Transformational leaders work to alter school culture by nurturing a professional learning community (Pan & Cheng, 2023). They serve as change agents or facilitators of change in order to actualize their vision for instructional excellence (Fullan, 2006; Rush, 2022). They work diligently and consistently to keep instructional quality as their main focus.

Transforming schools is easy if done superficially. Such change, however, is ephemeral. Unfortunately, much change, says Fullan (2003), occurs at this superficial level. In fact, he says, much of the change in schools in the 1960s around innovative instructional and curricular practices was short-lived because it was implemented on the surface without a deep change in people's beliefs and behavior. Both Fullan (2003) and Starratt (1995) concur that change without addressing a change in core beliefs and values is doomed to remain temporary and superficial. "Transformational leadership," says Starratt (1995), "is concerned with large, collective values" (p. 110). Leadership is predicated on the foundation of changing core beliefs and values.

Michael Fullan (1991, cited by Fullan, 2003) has identified:

> five crucial mind and action sets that leaders in the 21st century must cultivate: a deep sense of moral purpose, knowledge of the change process, capacity to develop relationships across diverse individuals and groups, skills in fostering knowledge creation and sharing, and the ability to engage with others in coherence making amidst multiple innovations. (p. 35)

1. *Engaging people's moral purposes:* School leaders do a good job setting the vision for students' social, emotional, and academic growth. Embedded in such a vision is a detailed articulation of the school's commitment to instructional excellence for all students. A school leader with such a vision is committed to refining the lives of children by improving the quality of the instruction they receive. Such a commitment is predicated on serving the needs of all students within an inclusive learning environment while remaining cognizant of extant research into the latest and most effective teaching pedagogies.
2. *Understand the change process:* Although Fullan discusses several ideas about change, I will highlight a few relevant ideas. The "implementation dip," according to Fullan, is a proverbial landmine. People, often board members, expect fast results. Fullan says, "Since change involves grappling with new beliefs and understandings, and new skills, competencies and behaviors, it is inevitable that it will not go smoothly in the early stages of implementation." Such an understanding helps people within the organization to relax and experiment with new ideas, practices, and policies. Learning anything new is initially "awkward."

Furthermore, being aware of this "implementation dip" actually shortens the dip, according to Fullan. Another aspect of change, for Fullan, is the realization of the necessity to overcome fear. Citing research by Black and Gregersen (2002 as cited by Fullan, 2006), Fullan explains the reason why despite a clear vision, people seem immobilized. He cites Black and Gregersen's answer:

> The clearer the new vision the easier it is for people to see all the specific ways in which they will be incompetent and look stupid. Many prefer to be competent at the [old] wrong thing than incompetent at the [new] right thing. (p. 69)

3. *Cultures for Learning:* This third mindset of change, according to Fullan, encourages the establishment of a conducive environment "so that people can learn from each other and become collectively committed to improvement." That is why involving teachers in decision-making about curriculum and instruction is so critical. Mechanisms and structures within a school need to be developed to allow for and facilitate communication among teachers and administrators about instruction. Instructional conversations, whether they take the form of lesson studies among members of the math department, "critical friends" teacher groups, action research projects by individual teachers, or supervisory strategies that encourage instructional dialogue about the proper use of wait time are at the heart of a professional learning community that values instructional improvement.

4. *Cultures of Evaluation:* Coupled with these emphases on instructional improvement is a focus on assessment. Gathering data on student learning continuously in aggregated and disaggregated ways and developing action plans based on an analysis of the data from parent, teacher, and student satisfaction surveys in order to inform instructional decision-making are examples of creating a culture of evaluation or assessment in a school. Fullan explains, "When schools . . . increase their collective capacity to engage in ongoing assessment for learning, major improvements are achieved." Citing Jim Collins (2002 cited by Fullan, 2007), he explains that "great organizations" have a "commitment to 'confronting the brutal facts' and establishing a culture of disciplined inquiry."

5. *Leadership for change:* Fullan asks, "What is the best leadership style for effecting the changes that are necessary in schools?" He explains, "It turns out that high-flying, charismatic leaders look like powerful change agents, but are actually bad for business because too much revolves around themselves." Leadership, he continues, must be distributed throughout the organization.

So what can school leaders glean from Fullan's advice? Strategically minded school leaders need to transform their work in schools deeply, not artificially and superficially. Doing so takes time and effort within a collaborative and empowering paradigm. A focus on the "Instructional Core" is fundamental and morally imperative, as emphasized in Chapter 2. Such work, moreover, is necessary because transformational leadership has been linked to student achievement, as discussed in Chapter 1. Cotton (2003), who has conducted one of the most extensive reviews of the literature in the field, states quite emphatically,

> Not surprisingly, researchers find that transformational leadership is positively related to student achievement and is more effective than the deal-making between principal and staff that characterizes the transactional approach alone. (p. 61)

In applying Fullan's work, school leaders need a moral commitment to follow through on the change initiatives. They need to ensure that teaching is more student-engaging with cycles of checking for understanding and feedback. The use of more formative assessments is necessary. School leaders need to involve teachers in curriculum development as well as the kind of PD best suited for them. They need to be conversant with alternatives to traditional supervision. Seeking ways to make teacher evaluation more effective so that it encourages teachers to improve their practice should be high on their agenda.

School leaders need the moral imperative to remain committed to instructional excellence by offering insights into ways our work in instruction can serve to enhance teachers' dignity, impact student learning, and transform their work, and in the process transform schools themselves, so that taken-for-granted educational practices turn into new opportunities and stagnation into transformation.[1]

CASE STUDY AND ITS ANALYSIS

Seaman High School located in the Midwest is an urban school with 65 teachers and 990 students in grades 9–12. Ninety-nine percent of the students go on to college. Among its peers, the school is considered to be academically rigorous, but it does offer leveled learning experiences for its diverse student body. The average years of experience among teachers is 15, with about 5 new teachers entering each year due to faculty retirements. The school is administered by four individuals, each with a different focus, that is, general, overall school administration (principal), student support (assistant principal), school-community liaison (assistant principal), and instructional coach.

The principal had just returned from Harvard University's Leadership Academy and wanted to transform his instructional program based on discussions and ideas he learned at the Academy. He was exposed to the literature on instructional transformation utilizing the most current pedagogical and supervisory strategies as well as cutting-edge educational practices.

Educational quality, he learned, is achieved to the extent to which those educators who work within the school are empowered to focus on instructional matters. For instance, even though the mentoring of new teachers is supported by research and best practice (Mullen & Fallen, 2022), his school as well as many others in Anywhere, USA, did not have a mentoring program in place for new teachers during their first three years of teaching.

Teachers at Seaman High School were divided, traditionally, by academic departments, each supervised by a chairperson. The academic culture in the school was traditional as personified by some of the following practices: curricula created in a top-down fashion, teacher evaluation based on yearly observations and write-ups, monthly faculty meetings focusing on disseminating information, and professional development opportunities primarily out-of-school, with occasional in-house workshops developed and conducted by administrators or outside consultants.

After months of planning with an Academy consultant, Dr. Cass, the principal decided to take action. With the assistance of a consultant, Dr. Cass shared his vision of change with the faculty, at formal meetings and informally daily. After the first year of visits by the consultant in which cutting-edge strategies of teaching, PD, and supervision were discussed, the school leadership team decided to seek volunteer teachers to begin on a small scale.

Eighteen teachers in three distinct academic departments volunteered to examine their teaching practices through the use of instructional leadership initiatives such as action research (Efron & Ravid, 2019), peer coaching (Robbins, 2015), critical friends (Cigdem Aktekin, 2014), book studies (Sullivan & Glanz, 2013) and/or instructional walk-throughs (McREL, 2019), all which aim to deepen the school's commitment to a culture of instructional excellence.

To actively engage teachers in nonthreatening ways to examine their practices in the classroom, Dr. Cass decided to provide the teachers with four options, initially, for reflective practice: book studies, walk-throughs, peer coaching, or action research. Whatever approach teachers would select, it would occur through self-initiation without oversight by a school administrator. Participants, though, would be asked at faculty or departmental meetings to share their reflective experiences without divulging any confidential matters among the teachers involved. The consultant, Amy Burroughs, a Harvard Leadership Academy experienced former principal and now consultant provided workshops on each option and allowed teachers to select one or more options (but no more than two at a time).

The change project continued for two years.

* * *

Learning Activity #1

Describe the challenges that Seaman High School faces to transform teaching and learning.

_____

_____

Research is clear that instructional change at the classroom level occurs within the context of a positive school culture that promotes a professional learning community in which professional development is primary (see, e.g., Klar et al., 2016). According to advocates, when all these domains work together then all those involved in the change become committed and motivated. The project at Seaman High School, described above and reported in Glanz (2016) in greater length, was successful in the long run, but challenges were readily apparent because it is difficult to change school culture quickly and teachers' teaching behaviors are engrained after years of conditioning.

The culture of teaching at Seaman High was based primarily on frontal teaching. Students were seated in traditional rows and many teachers used a lectern or podium to lecture at the front of the classroom. Recitation was evident in many situations wherein the teacher was most active, guiding lessons, posing questions in rapid succession, and calling randomly upon selected students. Many students during choral recitals (i.e., repeating in unison words or phrases uttered by the teacher first) were not engaged. The teacher's attention was focused on approximately 40 percent of the students in the class with most students' educational needs not attended to, a common problem with the overuse of frontal teaching (see the classic study by Hoetker & Ahllbrand, 1969).

Formative assessment, in general, was rarely applied. The use of pair and shares and other forms of formative assessments were, by and in large, not initially observed. Teachers at the school, for the most part, had not been exposed to pedagogies and technologies that allow for differentiation and alternate modalities or approaches of teaching including among others, pairs and shares, cooperative learning, reciprocal teaching, etc.

The faculty was given readings on cutting-edge teaching strategies. The teachers realized, of course, that the overuse of frontal teaching was common. Many of them initially supported it. One teacher explained, defensively, "How else is one to teach?" Another joined in, "We have large classes, a short amount of time, and much material to cover." Teachers in the English department, on the other hand, didn't seem perturbed by the recommendation to find alternatives to frontal teaching because they felt their classes were not overly frontal. "We incorporate active learning by encouraging students to read aloud and to role play," one English teacher explained.

Frontal teaching was most marked in specific departments such as science and mathematics. One teacher reacted somewhat harshly: "What do you mean we teach in a frontal manner, we conduct experiments with the students?!" Findings, though, demonstrated that although experiments were indeed conducted, they were, for the most part, performed by teachers themselves with most students looking on most of the time. It was after these discussions about the study's findings that we introduced action research as a means for teachers themselves to gather data to determine realities in the classroom, to see for themselves the manner in which they were teaching, and to possibly discover teaching alternatives, if they deemed them necessary.

At this point in the project, the volunteer teachers were asked to self-select a particular form of the instructional option. Some selected book studies (i.e., a group of usually no more than four or five teachers were to select a book to read and then discuss its implications among themselves), while others preferred collegial walk-throughs (short visits that focus on student work), or lesson studies, in which a team would create a lesson and then observe a colleague teaching it. A post conversation would later ensue among lesson participants.

The action research group, albeit small to start (six teachers; one later dropped out for health reasons) took their work seriously. At first, teachers in the action research group were eager to participate in learning about action research as it was a concept they were somewhat familiar with it in that some of them had attended previous seminars at local and national conferences on the subject. "Yeah," said one of the teachers, "at the conference, there were a bunch of sessions on action research and it sounded useful. . . . I mean, you get a chance to frame your own questions and ultimately see what is working, . . . or not." Another teacher posited, "A colleague at another school had mentioned that her principal gave teachers an option to either be observed formally by her or to do an action research project on their own. I think I'd opt for the latter."

None of the volunteers for the action research group, though, had ever used it to solve a real problem they faced in the classroom. School administrators designated specific times for teams to meet. Two times were most common: during common lunch periods and during daily preparation periods. Teachers in the action research group began to review the steps in action research (Glanz, 2005):

1. *Reflection:* Group members discussed at length the "claim" from the report that teaching was primarily frontal and that the needs of all learners weren't necessarily met using such an approach. Some representative comments included: "They [the administrators] are telling us that we have to focus on this perceived problem." "I think we have some leeway here to come up with an action research inquiry as long as it relates in some way to improving teaching." "No, we have to focus on the issue of overly frontal teaching." "The bottom line is what do we need to know to do a better job at teaching?" Much time was spent by the group reflecting and deciding on a focus for their action research projects. During this first phase, they also decided to examine some of the literature for ideas about alternatives to frontal teaching or ways to ensure that all students learn optimally during a given lesson.
2. *Select a Focus:* This step included discussion in three areas: (a) "knowing what we want to investigate," (b) "developing some questions about the area we've chosen," and (c) "establishing a plan to answer these questions." Representative comments included: "Let's come to an agreement on what aspect of our teaching we should focus on" and "Do we all have to focus on the same aspect like our questions and students' answers and how we react?" Much discussion continued without a clear focus agreed upon. They called the instructional coach for assistance. In the end, they reached a consensus that they'd focus on teacher-student interaction during questions-answers. They also came up with what they thought was a "novel, investigation."

    Based on material they had read from a Marshall Memo (see Appendix I), they examined the literature about the ecology of a classroom (e.g., table-chair arrangements impacting on student-teacher interaction during the lesson). "Yes," one of the teachers said, "let's focus on that aspect as well." One said, "I read that the way the desks and chairs in the room are set up influences, to some degree, the manner in which a teacher presents info." "Now that we have some focus, we need to phrase research questions and structure our study." They were discussing, and correctly so, the design phase of action research.
3. *Collect Data:* Once teachers had narrowed their focus to a few specific areas of concern, and had developed some research questions (e.g., "What impact does less lecturing and more student engagement; e.g., working in cooperative learning groups, problem-based learning, etc.) have on student motivational levels and achievement?" and

("What impact do alternative seating patterns to traditional rows have on teacher teaching behavior and student attentiveness?"), as well as make a plan to answer them, they appeared ready to gather information to answer their research questions. They decided to work in pairs with one teaching while the other observed to collect data. They decided to audio-record transactions, to be kept in confidence between them, and to video-record portions of the lesson to capture seating arrangements and other related interactions.

4. *Analyze and Interpret Data:* Once they collected relevant data, they began the process of analysis and interpretation to arrive at some decision/conclusions. At this juncture, much reflection and discussion occurred to make meaning of the data. First, pairs discussed each other's findings. Then they joined the others to compare data. Some representative comments included, "I tried to shorten my lecture to allow for more student input"; "I noticed that by seating them in groups rather than common rows that such an arrangement was more conducive to discussion, and, . . . very interesting, I tended to talk less seeing them sitting in groups"; "It seems a seating arrangement does break frontal teaching somewhat"; "But I still need to cover ground!"

5. *Take Action:* Finally, they reached the stage at which a decision had to be made. They answered their research questions about the effectiveness of their teaching in terms of limiting "frontalness." They found that talking less did encourage and engage students "more than ever before." They still had reservations, however, about the manner in which they would "cover ground, . . . complete the course of study . . . cover the curriculum." They also gathered some information about the seating arrangements in their rooms and their impact on teaching and students. They did find that seating students in horseshoe patterns or traditional groups proved more conducive to student-teacher engagement.

At this point in their deliberations, four possibilities existed in terms of the overall project: (a) they could somewhat modify their teaching based on their reflections and insights gained; (b) they could greatly modify their practices; (c) they could be somewhat dissatisfied with the results and therefore might reexamine their research questions and collect fresh data; or (d) they could disband the action research project, or modify it greatly. Action research, they knew, is cyclical and ongoing. The process didn't necessarily have to stop at any particular point. The information gained from previous research could open new avenues of research.

At this point, teachers were encouraged to consider some of the following questions that made the most sense to them:

1. What concerns me about the process?
2. Why am I concerned?
3. Can I confirm my perceptions?
4. What mistakes have I made?
5. If I were able to do it again, what would I do differently?
6. What are my current options?
7. What evidence can I collect to confirm my feelings?
8. Who might be willing to share their ideas with me?
9. What have been my successes?
10. How might I replicate these successes?
11. In what other ways might I improve my teaching?

Most of the troublesome areas during this implementation phase focused on administrative logistics, rather than interpersonal conflicts. For example, an email was received from the instructional coach as follows: "Action research teams had their recent meeting last week. Some grumbling about time and responsibilities. . . . Should I disband the team?" The team's complaints had essentially to do with administrative logistics and constraints on their time to do the job they wanted to do, that is, "to make it right."

Parenthetically, similar issues arose among other teams including the PD team and the clinical supervision team (although with the latter they had difficulty debriefing each other with sufficiently appropriate supportive language). The mentor program and the book studies group seemed to continue without any issues.

Teachers, although they still complained about "finding time to engage in reflection and the like," mentioned, "curiously" to one of them, that the "process, even though flawed at times, in the end, proved a useful means to examine their teaching." One team member reported, "I try to talk a bit less and engage students more with questions." Still, another reported, "Before I lecture on a topic, I do a K-W-L activity with them first to engage them for my talk." "I think I am less frontal; I don't know." No teacher could point to anything specific to demonstrate substantive changes in their teaching or student achievement levels. Most of their comments focused on some benefits of action research study such as, "This sort of research enabled me to see my classroom in ways I hadn't before." Three of the five reported that they "enjoyed planning and sharing with my colleague."

The major challenge to initiating instructional changes, at least in the early phase of the project, was premature initiation. The administration and department chairs at Seaman High were excited about developing alternatives to traditional supervision and evaluation. Several ideas were discussed. The school consultant was able to provide the school with an explanation and some PD in the interested areas: book studies, intervisitations, peer coaching, lesson studies, instructional rounds, action research, etc. In their eagerness, more than one model was initiated and thus confusion ensued. One AP explained as follows: "PD teams had their first meetings. Mentors and the book study group look like they are going to be crackerjack teams. Clinical rounds may be a social and logistical nightmare, but they could be productive with the right protocols and guidance." One teacher said, "We took on too much at the start."

Another example of premature initiation was not providing sufficient PD before initiating a strategy. Such a situation occurred with the instructional rounds group. Teachers seemed not to be able to distinguish between focusing on the process, rather than on the individual teacher. The aim was to avoid prescriptive and evaluative comments after observing a colleague teach. Rather, nonjudgmental descriptions of classroom interactions were optimal and preferred, as was introduced by the specialists during previous PD sessions. One representative teacher reported, "The clinical rounds team met today, and they wanted clearer guidelines on what they were looking for. They also were talking a language of evaluation even as they were aware that it was verboten."

Another teacher candidly said, "My gut reaction is that despite the potential benefits of rounds, culturally we are not ready for them yet. I can talk a good game about observing teaching but not teachers, but there are agendas built into observation protocols that will lead to judgments no matter how polite we are. What should we do?" It was suggested that they step back and have more discussion before implementation of current and future initiatives. One school administrator summarized participant's feelings: "We initiated too many projects at once."

Even though they knew that the literature supported a gradual implementation of new changes during an instructional reform effort (Cohen & Mehta, 2017), sometimes, at the initiation stage, excitement and overzealousness overtook participants. One teacher said, "I felt I just had to go along, . . . you know, don't rock the boat, . . . after all, others were enthusiastic; I just didn't feel that way." Also, as indicated by the literature, without attending to and transforming a school's culture which promotes a learning community and willingness to take risks, new instructional approaches are not anchored for success. Several teachers reported that "we are just used to the administration telling us what to do."

School administrators reflected, "Change isn't easy . . . you don't change a school overnight. . . . It's fine to strategically plan like we are but we must always keep in mind the morale of the faculty as well as our own." There were issues the school's administration had to grapple with as well (e.g., finding time in their schedules to handle instructional leadership initiatives, dealing with minor resistances, etc.).

Learning Activity #2

Describe the way you might have averted some of the challenges mentioned above:

_____

_____

LESSONS LEARNED

In closing, here are a few lessons divided into two categories:

1. General lessons about the nature of school reform:
   - Schools that are encouraged by their boards to improve are more likely to remain steadfast even as they encounter challenges and setbacks along the way.
   - Principals who provide sufficient support leadership are best at sustaining faculty interest in the specific reform.
   - Instructional improvement initiatives should be supported or nested within a larger strategic planning effort.
   - Resistance to change is common and should be expected.
   - Success is a multilayered, gradual process not always assured, but improvements, even though incremental, do occur.
   - Implement new changes slowly (even one at a time) and provide participants enough time to fully understand expectations and time to build requisite skills to ensure the success of strategy (e.g., use of action research).
2. Specific lessons about the use of action research by practitioners:
   - Action research naturally flows from the daily work of teachers because teachers inquisitively pose questions about the efficacy of their practice.
   - Although natural and based on common sense strategies, action research does require specific professional preparation to use it properly.
   - Teachers should read some of the abundant literature on action research work prior to project initiation.
   - Teachers should spend sufficient time (six months to a year) learning about action research before implementing it in their classrooms.
   - Support personnel should be readily available for teachers to consult when questions or problems arise.

- When working on action research projects, teachers, working in teams, should brainstorm questions for inquiry.
- Data should be collected from several different sources.
- Data interpretation, among teachers, needs to be guided by an action research specialist.
- Hire a specialist to oversee the entire process to provide situational assistance, as needed.
- When actions are taken by teachers in the classroom, their impact should be monitored carefully.
- Forums at which practitioners meet to share insights should be regularly planned.
- Reflection is the key skill and disposition most valuable in action research.

Changing and building a new culture of learning and improvement certainly takes time and continuous commitment. Remaining focused or as one school leader said, "Keeping your eye on the prize," makes good sense. Positive instructional change in any school is inevitably fraught with challenges. This school is still in the process of developing new ways of learning and improving.

REFERENCES

Cigdem Aktekin, N. (2014). *Teacher professional development: The Critical Friends Group (CFG).* Academic Publishing.

Cohen, D. K., & Mehta, J. D. (2017). Why reform sometimes succeeds: Understanding the conditions that produce reforms that last. *American Educational Research Journal, 54*(4), 644–690. http://www.jstor.org/stable/26641619

Cotton, K. (2003). *Principals and student achievement: What research says?* Association for Supervision and Curriculum Development.

Efron, E., & Ravid, S. (2019). *Action research in education: A practical guide* (2nd ed.). The Guilford Press.

Fullan, M. (2003). *Change forces with a vengeance.* Routledge Falmer.

Fullan, M. (2006). *Turnaround leadership.* Jossey-Bass.

Fullan, M. (2007). *The new meaning of educational change* (4th ed.). Teachers College Press.

Fullan, M. (2008). *The six secrets of change.* Jossey-Bass.

Glanz, J. (2005). Action research as instructional leadership: Suggestions for principals. *National Association of Secondary School Principals Bulletin (NASSP Bulletin), 89*(643), 17–27. http://doi.org/10.1177/019263650508964303

Glanz, J. (2016). Action research by practitioners: A case study of a high school's attempt to create transformational change. *Journal of Practitioner Research, 1*(1), Article 3. http://doi.org/10.5038/2379-9951.1.1.1027

Johnson, C. C., & Fargo, J. D. (2010). Urban school reform enabled by transformative professional development: Impact on teacher change and student learning of science. *Urban Education, 45*(1), 4–29. https://doi.org/10.1177/0042085909352073

Hoetker, J., & Ahlbrand Jr., W. P. (1969). The persistence of the recitation. *American Educational Research Journal, 6*(2), 145–167. http://doi.org/10.2307/30034819

Klar, H. W., Huggins, K. S., & Roessler, A. P. (2016). Fostering distributed instructional leadership: A strategy for supporting teacher learning. In J. Glanz & S. J. Zepeda (Eds.), *Supervision: New perspectives in theory and practice.* Rowman & Littlefield.

McREL. (2019). The value of classroom walkthroughs: One district's perspective. https://www.mcrel.org/value-of-classroom-walkthroughs/

Mullen, C. A., & Fallen, M. S. (2022). Navigating uncharted waters: New teacher mentoring and induction. *Research in Educational Administration and Leadership, 7*(4). https://dergipark.org.tr/tr/download/article-file/2610799

Pan, H.-L.W, & Cheng, S.-H. (2023). Examining the impact of teacher learning communities on self-efficacy and professional learning: An application of the theory-driven evaluation. *Sustainability, 15*, 4771. https://doi.org/10.3390/su15064771

Robbins, P. (2015). *Peer coaching to enrich professional practice, school culture, and student learning.* Association for Supervision and Curriculum Development.

Rush, P. (2022, March 31). The principal as a change agent. *Tui Tuia Learning Circle.* https://www.learningcircle.co.nz/blog/the-principal-as-a-change-agent

Sarason, S. (1982). *The culture of the school and the problem of change* (2nd ed.). Allyn & Bacon.

Starratt, R. J. (1995). *Leaders with vision: The quest for school renewal.* Corwin.

Sullivan, S., & Glanz, J. (2013). *Supervision that improves teaching: Strategies and techniques* (4th ed.). Corwin.

NOTE

1. Some readers will complain that although the ideas in this book are intriguing, they are, for the most part, unrealistic because of the difficulty to find the time to devote to promoting instructional quality. I maintain that if a school leader, or anyone in a position of influencing instructional quality is committed to instructional improvement they will find the time. Allocating an hour in the morning and, say, 45 minutes in the afternoon for uninterrupted time to work with teachers on curriculum or observe and provide feedback to a teacher is not impossible. Some principals I know block off time in their schedule and inform their secretary that barring an emergency, "I am not to be disturbed." There are several no-cost or very low-cost measures that can be taken as well to make such work a reality. For instance, some school leaders incorporate such strategies: Lunch and learns (i.e., catering lunches,

from time to time, with or for teachers to discuss instructional issues), devoting most faculty meetings to focus on instruction, hiring substitutes to relieve selected teachers on a rotational basis to attend a curriculum discussion with a small group of peers, etc.

Appendix A

State of Teaching, Curriculum, Professional Development, Supervision, and Evaluation (Shortest Version) Questionnaire

Based on your own experiences in the school system in which you work or have worked, please respond to these questions. Submission of this questionnaire demonstrates your consent to partake in the study. Your identity is secure.

Country(ies) on which you are basing your responses:
_____

Check one or more on which you are basing your responses:
___ Preschool
___ Elementary school (grades K–5)
___ Middle school (grades 6–8)
___ High school (grades 9–12)

Type of school:
___ Public or government
___ Secular private or independent
___ Religious private or independent
___ Other; specify _____

Check your position(s) on which you are basing your responses:
___ Classroom teacher
___ Teacher leader
___ Assistant principal

___ Principal
___ Any other kind of supervisor/mentor
___ School/system-affiliated political leader
___ Ministry or department of education official
___ Professor of education
___ Other; please specify: _____

If you wish to obtain the results of this survey, please record your email address:

_____

For each statement below, indicate the extent to which you agree or disagree with the statement by circling the appropriate number.

4 – SA = Strongly Agree ("For the most part, yes")
3 – A = Agree ("Yes, but . . . ")
2 – D = Disagree ("No, but . . . ")
1 – SD = Strongly Disagree ("For the most part, no")
? – Don't know

	SA	A	D	SD	?
1. Teachers are generally consulted, in advance, regarding the topics they perceive they need for professional development.	4	3	2	1	?
2. Professional development is usually ongoing, discipline-based, differentiated, and helpful.	4	3	2	1	?
3. Curriculum development is generally a collaborative process involving teachers.	4	3	2	1	?
4. Teachers have a say in the criteria used in teacher evaluation.	4	3	2	1	?
5. From my experience, teachers mostly lecture (talk) to students without enough student participation.	4	3	2	1	?
6. Principals rarely provide appropriate and meaningful feedback to teachers.	4	3	2	1	?
7. The ministry or department of education in my country, operates in a top-down fashion, with little input from school personnel.	4	3	2	1	?
8. Principals find it difficult to change the culture of the school to which they were appointed because of ministry/department of education policies.	4	3	2	1	?
9. Principals, generally, are more managers than they are instructional leaders.	4	3	2	1	?

10. It's my impression that the Ministry or Board of Education gives principals lots of leeway in developing curriculum.	4	3	2	1	?
11. Most teachers would report that teacher evaluation in the school is not very useful for improving teaching.	4	3	2	1	?
12. Judging teacher competence is usually a fair process in schools.	4	3	2	1	?
13. The curriculum in my school or district is mapped and well-organized.	4	3	2	1	?
14. Most principals would say they can't find the time to work with teachers on improving teaching in the classroom.	4	3	2	1	?
15. Walk-throughs by principals are commonly employed wherein they pop in to observe classrooms with little or any substantive feedback given to teachers.	4	3	2	1	?
16. Alternatives to traditional supervision (i.e., direct observations) such as instructional rounds, lesson studies, intervisitations, peer coaching, and reflective journaling, are rarely found.	4	3	2	1	?
17. Most teachers would affirm that they receive constructive feedback from their principals on a fairly regular basis.	4	3	2	1	?
18. Teachers are given feedback about their teaching in a descriptive rather than judgmental manner in order to stimulate conversation about their teaching.	4	3	2	1	?
19. PISA and other international assessment test results are accurate measures to determine the quality of instruction in schools. In other words, schools with the highest results can be characterized as having high instructional quality.	4	3	2	1	?
20. Outdated curricula and overuse of prepackaged curricula are too prevalent in schools.	4	3	2	1	?

Feel free to add additional comments on any particular item(s) in this questionnaire, or any other general (or specific) comments about the nature and quality of instruction in classrooms/schools in your country.

_____

_____

_____

_____

_____
_____

Please append other comments.

Appendix B

State of Teaching, Curriculum, Professional Development, Supervision, and Evaluation (Short Version) Questionnaire

Based on your own experiences in the school system in which you work or have worked, please respond to these questions. Submission of this questionnaire demonstrates your consent to partake in the study. Your identity is secure.

Country(ies) on which you are basing your responses:

_____

Check one or more on which you are basing your responses:
- ___ Preschool
- ___ Elementary school (grades K–5)
- ___ Middle school (grades 6–8)
- ___ High school (grades 9–12)

Type of school:
- ___ Public or government
- ___ Secular private or independent
- ___ Religious private or independent
- ___ Other; specify _____

Check your position(s) on which you are basing your responses:
- ___ Classroom teacher
- ___ Teacher leader
- ___ Assistant principal

___ Principal
___ Any other kind of supervisor/mentor
___ School/system-affiliated political leader
___ Ministry or department of education official
___ Professor of education
___ Other; please specify: _____

If you wish to obtain the results of this survey, please record your email address:

_____

For each statement below, indicate the extent to which you agree or disagree with the statement by circling the appropriate number.

4 – SA = Strongly Agree ("For the most part, yes")
3 – A = Agree ("Yes, but . . . ")
2 – D = Disagree ("No, but . . . ")
1 – SD = Strongly Disagree ("For the most part, no")
? – Don't know

	SA	A	D	SD	?
1. Most teachers know how to make instructional modifications for students who need assistance.	4	3	2	1	?
2. Most principals see themselves as instructional leaders.	4	3	2	1	?
3. Teachers, by in large, would report that they have support from their supervisor(s) to try new ideas and implement creative pedagogy.	4	3	2	1	?
4. Teachers are generally consulted, in advance, regarding the topics they perceive they need for professional development.	4	3	2	1	?
5. Professional development is usually ongoing, discipline-based, and differentiated.	4	3	2	1	?
6. Most teachers would report: "Opportunities for professional development are provided by my school/district that meet my needs."	4	3	2	1	?
7. Curriculum development is generally a collaborative process involving teachers.	4	3	2	1	?
8. Teachers have a say about the criteria used in teacher evaluation.	4	3	2	1	?
9. From my experience, teachers mostly lecture (talk) to students without enough student participation.	4	3	2	1	?

Appendix B

10. Principals rarely provide appropriate and meaningful feedback to teachers.	4 3 2 1 ?
11. Teachers would report: "I am knowledgeable and skillful at differentiating instruction."	4 3 2 1 ?
12. Teachers employ formative assessments to check for understanding on a regular, consistent basis.	4 3 2 1 ?
13. The ministry or department of education in my country operates in a top-down fashion, with little input from school personnel.	4 3 2 1 ?
14. Principals find it difficult to change the culture of the school to which they were appointed because of ministry/department of education policies.	4 3 2 1 ?
15. Most teachers use wait time effectively.	4 3 2 1 ?
16. Principals, generally, are more managers than they are instructional leaders.	4 3 2 1 ?
17. Teachers, generally, would state that their principal provides instructional support for them on a consistent, meaningful basis.	4 3 2 1 ?
18. Teaching is viewed, by most school leaders, as a process of giving over information to students.	4 3 2 1 ?
19. Summative assessment is more often employed by teachers in the classroom than formative assessments.	4 3 2 1 ?
20. Professional development is episodic, noncollaborative, and not usually useful.	4 3 2 1 ?
21. It's my impression that the ministry or board of education gives principals lots of leeway in developing curriculum.	4 3 2 1 ?
22. Most teachers would report that teacher evaluation in the school is not very useful as a means to improve teaching.	4 3 2 1 ?
23. State-mandated curricula standards are generally welcomed by most principals.	4 3 2 1 ?
24. State-mandated curricula standards are generally welcomed by most teachers.	4 3 2 1 ?
25. Judging teacher competence is usually a fair process in schools.	4 3 2 1 ?
26. Curricular standards are mainly imposed "from above," with little ability for teachers to revise curricula.	4 3 2 1 ?
27. The curriculum in my school or district is mapped and well-organized.	4 3 2 1 ?
28. Principals frequently visit classroom to offer instructional assistance.	4 3 2 1 ?
29. Most principals would say they can't find the time to work with teachers on improving teaching in the classroom.	4 3 2 1 ?

30. Before most observations, a preconference and a post-conference are held between the teacher and the principal.	4 3 2 1 ?
31. Mentoring and/or teacher induction programs for first-year teachers are commonly employed in most schools.	4 3 2 1 ?
32. Most teachers would say that has professional development helped improve teaching practices.	4 3 2 1 ?
33. Walk-throughs by principals are commonly employed wherein they pop in to observe classrooms with little or any substantive feedback given to teachers.	4 3 2 1 ?
34. Alternatives to traditional supervision (i.e., direct observations) such as instructional rounds, lesson studies, intervisitations, peer coaching, and reflective journaling, are rarely found.	4 3 2 1 ?
35. Most teachers would affirm that they receive constructive feedback from their principals on a fairly regular basis.	4 3 2 1 ?
36. Teachers are given feedback about their teaching in a descriptive rather than judgmental manner in order to stimulate conversation about their teaching.	4 3 2 1 ?
37. Teachers would report: "I am satisfied with the way I am evaluated by my principal."	4 3 2 1 ?
38. Most professional development initiatives encourage and provide teachers with relevant and practical books and materials to further their knowledge and skills.	4 3 2 1 ?
39. PISA and other international assessment test results are accurate measures to determine the quality of instruction in schools. In other words, schools with the highest results can be characterized as having high instructional quality.	4 3 2 1 ?
40. The persistence of recitation (i.e., teachers talk, and students listen) is all too common at all levels of schooling.	4 3 2 1 ?
41. Outdated curricula and overuse of prepackaged curricula are too prevalent in schools.	4 3 2 1 ?
42. Mandated professional development (PD) is viewed by most teachers as irrelevant and boring.	4 3 2 1 ?
43. Teacher evaluation is perceived by most teachers as unfair, subjective, and arbitrary.	4 3 2 1 ?
44. Supervision of instruction conducted by principals, or their representatives is viewed by most teachers as inspectional, rather than helpful.	4 3 2 1 ?
45. Ministries or departments of education mandate school policies without the participation of teachers and/or principals.	4 3 2 1 ?

Appendix B 101

Feel free to add additional comments on any particular item(s) in this questionnaire, or any other general (or specific) comments about the nature and quality of instruction in classrooms/schools in your country.

_____
_____
_____
_____
_____

Please append other comments.

Appendix C

State of Teaching, Curriculum, Professional Development, Supervision, and Evaluation (Long Version) Questionnaire

Based on your own experiences in the school system in which you work or have worked, please respond to these questions. Submission of this questionnaire demonstrates your consent to partake in the study. Your identity is secure.

Country(ies) on which you are basing your responses:

_____

Check one or more on which you are basing your responses:
 ___ Preschool
 ___ Elementary school (grades K–5)
 ___ Middle school (grades 6–8)
 ___ High school (grades 9–12)

Type of school:
 ___ Public or government
 ___ Secular private or independent
 ___ Religious private or independent
 ___ Other; specify _____

Check your position(s) on which you are basing your responses:
 ___ Classroom teacher
 ___ Teacher leader
 ___ Assistant principal

___ Principal
___ Any other kind of supervisor/mentor
___ School/system-affiliated political leader
___ Ministry or department of education official
___ Professor of education
___ Other; please specify: _____

If you wish to obtain the results of this survey, please record your email address:
_____

Part One: For each statement below, indicate the extent to which you agree or disagree with the statement by circling the appropriate number.
4 – SA = Strongly Agree ("For the most part, yes")
3 – A = Agree ("Yes, but . . . ")
2 – D = Disagree ("No, but . . . ")
1 – SD = Strongly Disagree ("For the most part, no")
? – Don't know

	SA A D SD ?
1. Most principals know how to facilitate best practices in teaching, curriculum, and supervision.	4 3 2 1 ?
2. Most principals spend significant time on the job working with teachers in a collegial fashion to improve teaching practices.	4 3 2 1 ?
3. Teachers know how to make instructional modifications for students who need assistance.	4 3 2 1 ?
4. Principals see themselves as instructional leaders	4 3 2 1 ?
5. Teachers, by and large, are well-prepared and display solid content knowledge.	4 3 2 1 ?
6. Teachers, by and large, are well-prepared and display solid pedagogical knowledge.	4 3 2 1 ?
7. Teachers, by and large, differentiate instruction in their classrooms.	4 3 2 1 ?
8. Principals are familiar with learning styles and multiple intelligences theories and can help teachers apply them to instructional practices.	4 3 2 1 ?
9. Teachers would report that they have support from their supervisor(s) to try new ideas and implement creative pedagogy.	4 3 2 1 ?

10. Principals are generally familiar with curricular and teaching resources to assist teachers.	4	3	2	1	?
11. Teachers incorporate a systematic plan for assessment of student learning.	4	3	2	1	?
12. Teachers are consulted, in advance, regarding the topics they perceive they need for professional development.	4	3	2	1	?
13. Professional development is ongoing, discipline-based, and differentiated.	4	3	2	1	?
14. Teacher interactions with students are generally friendly and demonstrate warmth and caring.	4	3	2	1	?
15. Teachers are expected to develop a system of discipline without a supervisor's assistance.	4	3	2	1	?
16. Teachers would report: "Opportunities for staff development are provided by my school that meet my needs for professional growth."	4	3	2	1	?
17. Most principals delegate instructional leadership initiatives to an assistant.	4	3	2	1	?
18. Curriculum development is a collaborative process involving teachers.	4	3	2	1	?
19. Curriculum development is a collaborative process involving parents, when appropriate.	4	3	2	1	?
20. Teachers have a say about the criteria used in teacher evaluation.	4	3	2	1	?
21. From my experience, teachers mostly lecture (talk) to students without enough student participation.	4	3	2	1	?
22. Principals rarely provide appropriate and meaningful feedback to teachers.	4	3	2	1	?
23. Teachers would report: "I am knowledgeable and skillful at differentiating instruction."	4	3	2	1	?
24. Teachers are consistently encouraged to seek advice from their principal on teaching and learning matters.	4	3	2	1	?
25. Teachers employ formative assessments to check for understanding on a regular, consistent basis.	4	3	2	1	?
26. Ministries or departments of education in most countries operate in a top-down fashion, with little input from school personnel.	4	3	2	1	?
27. Teachers are usually given an understanding of what the principal or designee expects during an observation.	4	3	2	1	?
28. Principals find it difficult to change the culture of the school to which they were appointed because of ministry/department of education policies.	4	3	2	1	?

29. Teachers use wait time effectively.	4 3 2 1 ?
30. Principals, generally, as more managers than they are instructional leaders.	4 3 2 1 ?
31. Most teachers cannot teach to different student learning styles.	4 3 2 1 ?
32. Most principals collaborate with teachers in a cordial and professional manner.	4 3 2 1 ?
33. Teachers, generally, would state that their supervisor provides instructional support for them on a consistent, meaningful basis.	4 3 2 1 ?
34. Teaching is viewed, by most supervisors, as a process of giving over information to students.	4 3 2 1 ?
35. Teachers are encouraged to serve on a school-based curriculum committee.	4 3 2 1 ?
36. Teachers have a solid understanding of learning styles and multiple intelligences theories and can apply them to instructional practice.	4 3 2 1 ?
37. Principals view themselves as "teachers of teachers."	4 3 2 1 ?
38. Principals have a solid understanding of learning styles and multiple intelligences theories and can apply them to instructional practice.	4 3 2 1 ?
39. Summative assessment is more often employed by teachers in the classroom than formative assessments.	4 3 2 1 ?
40. Teachers are respected as educational professionals.	4 3 2 1 ?
41. During a given lesson, most students do not actively participate in class discussions.	4 3 2 1 ?
42. Teachers feel threatened by supervisors.	4 3 2 1 ?
43. Teachers feel lines of communication between principal and teachers are open.	4 3 2 1 ?
44. Professional development is episodic, noncollaborative, and not usually useful.	4 3 2 1 ?
45. The ministry or board of education gives principals lots of leeway in developing curriculum.	4 3 2 1 ?
46. The ministry or board of education is highly bureaucratic creating a top-down decision-making process.	4 3 2 1 ?
47. Teachers would report that teacher evaluation in the school is not very useful as a means to improve teaching.	4 3 2 1 ?
48. State-mandated curricula standards are welcomed by most principals.	4 3 2 1 ?
49. Supervisors are familiar with the research on the use of wait time.	4 3 2 1 ?

50. State-mandated curricula standards are welcomed by most teachers.	4 3 2 1 ?
51. According to my understanding, the manner in which the supervision of instruction is practiced in schools is similar to how it is practiced in most other schools in different countries.	4 3 2 1 ?
52. Principals are managers first, and instructional leaders second.	4 3 2 1 ?
53. Judging teacher competence is a fair process in this school.	4 3 2 1 ?
54. Curricular standards are mainly imposed from above, with little ability for teachers to revise curricula.	4 3 2 1 ?
55. Most professional development offered to teachers is focused on student learning.	4 3 2 1 ?
56. The curriculum is mapped and well-organized.	4 3 2 1 ?
57. Parents are partners in instruction and are encouraged to participate in this school.	4 3 2 1 ?
58. The curriculum in this school is written, discussed, understood, and revised every few years.	4 3 2 1 ?
59. Teachers would report: "I have an opportunity on occasion to visit my colleagues as they teach."	4 3 2 1 ?
60. Principals frequently visit my classroom to offer instructional assistance.	4 3 2 1 ?
61. Teachers would report: "I receive adequate resources to support instruction, especially in technology."	4 3 2 1 ?
62. Release time is provided for professional development and additional preparation to improve teaching.	4 3 2 1 ?
63. Professional growth plans are developed on an annual basis between principals and teachers.	4 3 2 1 ?
64. Supervisors understand that effective teachers actively engage their students, check student understanding, and provide meaningful feedback to students.	4 3 2 1 ?
65. Teachers are invited to review and revise curricula.	4 3 2 1 ?
66. Most supervisors have never heard of the concept known as the "Instructional Core," which states that learning occurs in the interaction among three components: "What teachers are doing and saying?" "What students are doing and saying in response to teacher behavior," and "What is the task at hand (i.e., content activity)?"	4 3 2 1 ?
67. There is an opportunity to meet with my supervisor about my teaching practice.	4 3 2 1 ?
68. Curriculum materials are readily available in the school.	4 3 2 1 ?

69. Teacher evaluation is used to threaten teachers.	4 3 2 1 ?
70. Teachers feel threatened by supervisors.	4 3 2 1 ?
71. Faculty opinions are solicited but seldom used.	4 3 2 1 ?
72. Judging teacher competence is a fair process in this school.	4 3 2 1 ?
73. Most principals would say they can't find the time to work with teachers on improving teaching in the classroom.	4 3 2 1 ?
74. State-mandated curricula standards are perceived as onerous and restrictive by most principals.	4 3 2 1 ?
75. Before most observations, a preconference and a post conference are held between the teacher and the supervisor.	4 3 2 1 ?
76. In the teaching of reading, oral reading (i.e., calling on students to read aloud while other classmates listen/read along) is common practice in schools.	4 3 2 1 ?
77. Principals are conversant about constructivist theory.	4 3 2 1 ?
78. Teachers are conversant and utilize constructivist theory in planning and conducting lessons.	4 3 2 1 ?
79. Mentoring and/or teacher induction programs for first-year teachers are commonly employed in most schools.	4 3 2 1 ?
80. Teachers are actively encouraged to use action research to address classroom issues or problems.	4 3 2 1 ?
81. Most teachers would say that professional development has helped improve teaching practices.	4 3 2 1 ?
82. Principals use supervision as a means to assess a teacher's teaching competence.	4 3 2 1 ?
83. Principals also use action research to gather data to inform decision-making or solve problems.	4 3 2 1 ?
84. Walk-throughs by supervisors are commonly employed wherein they pop in to observe classrooms with little or any substantive feedback given to teachers.	4 3 2 1 ?
85. Most principals I know are very knowledgeable and use clinical supervision with their teachers.	4 3 2 1 ?
86. Peer coaching is commonly practiced in schools.	4 3 2 1 ?
87. State-mandated curriculum standards are perceived as onerous and restrictive by most teachers.	4 3 2 1 ?
88. Alternatives to traditional supervision (i.e., direct observations) such as instructional rounds, lesson studies, intervisitations, and reflective journaling, are rarely found.	4 3 2 1 ?
89. Teachers would affirm that they receive constructive feedback from their supervisors on a fairly regular basis.	4 3 2 1 ?

90. Faculty meetings, conducted after or during school, mostly focus on administrative matters that could easily have been communicated via a memo or email.	4 3 2 1 ?
91. Teachers are consulted in advance about topics they would like addressed at faculty meetings.	4 3 2 1 ?
92. Teachers are given feedback about their teaching in a descriptive rather than judgmental manner in order to stimulate conversation about their teaching.	4 3 2 1 ?
93. Principals are the ones who determine what is to be observed during a formal observation.	4 3 2 1 ?
94. Supervisors say, by and large, that it's difficult to find the time to give teacher supervision the time that it demands.	4 3 2 1 ?
95. Principals are selected for their pedagogical knowledge and instructional leadership capabilities.	4 3 2 1 ?
96. Teachers understand the connection between constructivism and its relation to differentiation.	4 3 2 1 ?
97. Principals understand the connection between constructivism and its relation to differentiation.	4 3 2 1 ?
98. Decision-making in schools can be described as democratic.	4 3 2 1 ?
99. Principals would report: "I receive most of what I need to run my school from the ministry/board/department."	4 3 2 1 ?
100. Teachers are involved with their supervisors about what is considered "good teaching."	4 3 2 1 ?
101. Teachers would report: "I am satisfied with the way I am evaluated by my principal."	4 3 2 1 ?
102. The ministry/board/department encourages principals to implement their own reforms in their schools.	4 3 2 1 ?
103. Most educators perceive their ministries/boards/departments as bureaucratic and would decry the waste and needless paperwork required.	4 3 2 1 ?
104. The ministry/board/department supports (via e.g., funds, materials) principals to implement their own reforms in their schools.	4 3 2 1 ?
105. Principals encourage teachers to offer suggestions to implement change/reforms in the school.	4 3 2 1 ?
106. Professional development initiatives encourage and provide teachers with relevant and practical books and materials to further their knowledge and skills.	4 3 2 1 ?
107. Teachers would report that there is a learning culture in their schools.	4 3 2 1 ?

108. Most would concur that principals must have been teachers, with at least about three years of experience, prior to assuming the principalship.	4	3	2	1	?
109. I believe that hiring teachers with the best college grade point averages as well as the highest scores on accepted standardized achievement tests is among the most significant factors for improving instructional quality in the classroom.	4	3	2	1	?
110. PISA and other international assessment test results are accurate measures to determine the quality of instruction in schools. In other words, schools with the highest results indicate high instructional quality.	4	3	2	1	?

Feel free to add additional comments on any particular item(s) in this questionnaire or any other general comments about assessing instructional quality in classrooms.

Please append other comments.

Part Two:

I would appreciate you completing the following questions. Please copy/paste each item in a separate Word document to respond, OR you can consent to an interview with me in which I will ask you these questions:

1. Based on your knowledge, observations, and experiences in schools in your country, please react to the following statements in terms of the degree to which the statements represent or describe schools, in general. I would appreciate if you could at least write, briefly, a narrative, perhaps with real-life examples to support your statements:
    a. The persistence of recitation (i.e., teachers talk, and students listen) is all too common at all levels of schooling.
    b. Outdated curricula or overuse of prepackaged curricula is too prevalent in schools.
    c. Mandated professional development is viewed by most teachers as irrelevant and boring.
    d. Teacher evaluation is perceived by teachers as unfair, subjective, and arbitrary.
    e. Supervision of instruction by school leaders is viewed by teachers as inspectional, rather than helpful.

f. Ministries or departments of education mandate school policies without the participation of teachers and/or principals.
g. Creating school-wide instructional change is a difficult, if not impossible, task given the unique constraints imposed by the board/ministry of education.

Appendix D
On-the-Spot Beliefs about Instructional Quality Questionnaire

Directions: Beliefs influence our conception of leadership and consequently our actions (Osterman & Kottkamp, 2015). This questionnaire challenges readers to reflect on views of leadership with particular attention to instructional leadership. Research indicates that the extent to which school leaders attend to instructional matters within the classroom is influenced in large measure by their beliefs of efficacy regarding their work in instructional leadership (Blasé & Blasé, 2004; Sullivan & Glanz, 2013). Using the Likert-scale questionnaire below, circle the answer that best represents your on-the-spot belief about each statement. After the survey, I include a brief discussion on each of the items. Readers may agree or disagree with my responses, but I hope they will provoke reflection and continued study.

SA = Strongly Agree ("For the most part, yes")
A = Agree ("Yes, but . . . ")
D = Disagree ("No, but . . . ")
SD = Strongly Disagree ("For the most part, no")

SA A D SD   1. To be effective, the principal must have been a successful classroom teacher.

SA A D SD   2. Good principals must know how to facilitate best practices in teaching, curriculum, and supervision.

SA A D SD   3. It is reasonable to expect a principal to serve as a presenter in a professional development session.

SA A D SD   4. It is reasonable to expect principals to know as much or more about wait time, Bloom's Taxonomy, and differentiated instruction as do teachers.

SA A D SD   5. It is reasonable to expect principals to lead disciplinary instruction in mathematics, biology, English, history, etc.

SA A D SD   6. The principal should spend many hours on the job in the classroom each day.

SA A D SD   7. The principal should be the most important instructional leader in a school.

SA A D SD   8. The principal is the single greatest factor in determining the extent of student achievement.

SA A D SD   9. Instructional leadership should take priority over other forms of leadership.

SA A D SD   10. I am comfortable facilitating instructional leadership in my school.

Suggested responses:
1. To be effective, the principal must have been a successful classroom teacher.
   Successful, yes. Not necessarily the best.
2. Good principals must know how to facilitate best practices in teaching, curriculum, and supervision.
   Yes, and "facilitate" is the keyword.
3. It is reasonable to expect a principal to serve as a presenter in a professional development session.
   Yes. Not the sole presenter, but a principal should feel comfortable enough to "show the way" by demonstrating sound teaching practices; to communicate to others "Do as I do, not just as I say."
4. It is reasonable to expect principals to know as much or more about wait time, Bloom's Taxonomy, and differentiated instruction as do teachers.
   No. Although principals are somewhat conversant with ideas in each area, they are not experts and should therefore reach out to others; the principal serves here as a discussant of these areas with teachers.
5. It is reasonable to expect principals to lead disciplinary instruction in mathematics, biology, English, history, etc.

No. The words of Wilmore (2004) are instructive here: "Yet even though you are the instructional leader, there is nothing that requires you to be the expert in all forms of language, mathematics, science, technology, history, and civic responsibility. What you are required to do is to understand and facilitate appropriate processes for curriculum enhancement and developmentally appropriate instructional methods. . . . You are the facilitator of these areas, not the sole provider of them" (p. 51).

6. The principal should spend many hours on the job in the classroom each day.

   Not necessarily. Although a principal who believes and feels comfortable in dealing with instructional matters spends a large part of the day thinking about and facilitating instruction, it is equally unreasonable that the principal needs to spend literally hours in the classroom. Although, you will notice that principals who have not been successful teachers and are uncomfortable and/or not knowledgeable about teaching, for instance, will avoid the classroom or spend just a few moments "shooting the breeze" with teachers and students in the classroom.

7. The principal should be the most important instructional leader in a school.

   Yes, but not the sole leader. Allow me to quote Wilmore (2004) once again: "Be careful to notice the difference between being able to facilitate the successful progress of teachers and others, rather than doing everything yourself. If you try to do that, you will kill yourself. Once dead, there isn't anything you can do to help anyone, so budget your time" (p. 51).

8. The principal is the single greatest factor in determining the extent of student achievement.

   Yes and no. Promoting student achievement is a complex process that involves many school/classroom/community contextual variables. Although the teacher is certainly the key individual in the classroom, who on a daily basis influences student learning, the principal can be viewed as an orchestra leader of sorts who coordinates, facilitates, and oversees the instructional process on a school-wide basis. The principal as an orchestra leader, seen in this way, is the most important link or ingredient to ensure high student achievement.

9. Instructional leadership should take priority over other forms of leadership.

   All forms of leadership work in synchronicity, that is, in unison with one another. Although it is difficult to separate instructional from cultural leadership and other forms of leadership, the principal, I assert, should be primarily focused strategically on promoting high instructional standards that encourage exceptional teaching, yielding high achievement for all students.

10. I am comfortable facilitating instructional leadership in my school.

    This is a statement each of you must assess on your own. If you have not had successful or sufficient experience in the classroom, all is not lost. You must engage in strong and ongoing personal and professional development in this area. The more you read, the more workshops you attend, and the more you practice your instructional skills, the more legitimacy you'll receive in the eyes of teachers and the more likely you'll positively influence the school's instructional program (i.e., have an impact on teaching, PD, curriculum, supervision, and evaluation).

REFERENCES

Blase, J., & Blase, J. (2004). *Handbook of instructional leadership: How successful principals promote teaching and learning.* Corwin.

Osterman, K. E., & Kottkamp, R. B. (2015). *Reflective practice for educators: Professional development to improve student learning.* Corwin.

Sullivan, S., & Glanz, J. (2013). *Supervision that improves teaching: Strategies and techniques* (4th ed.). Corwin.

Wilmore, E. L. (2004). *Principal induction: A standards-based model for administrator development.* Corwin.

Appendix E

Assessing Your Role as an Instructional Leader and Supervisor Questionnaire

In *Enhancing Professional Practice: A Framework for Teaching* (2007) published by the Association for Supervision and Curriculum Development, Charlotte Danielson developed a framework or model for understanding teaching based on current research in the field. She identified "components" clustered into four domains of teaching responsibility: planning and preparation, classroom environment, instruction, and professional responsibilities. I adapted and developed the questionnaire below based on her framework. Please take the survey now because it will serve as an important reflective tool to consider the areas that are instructionally important to you. Please note that your responses are private. Therefore, your honest responses to the various items below will best serve as reflective tools to assist you in becoming an even better instructional leader. At the end, you will find a brief self-analysis to encourage reflection on your role as an instructional leader.

SA = Strongly Agree ("For the most part, yes")
A = Agree ("Yes, but . . . ")
D = Disagree ("No, but . . . ")
SD = Strongly Disagree ("For the most part, no")

Planning and Preparation

SA A D SD   1. Teachers should be offered guidance in planning and preparing for instruction, and I feel comfortable in doing so.

SA A D SD   2. Good teachers should display solid content knowledge and connect with the parts of their discipline or other disciplines.

SA A D SD   3. Good teachers should consider the importance of prerequisite knowledge when introducing new topics.

SA A D SD   4. Good teachers actively build on students' prior knowledge and seek causes for students' misunderstandings.

SA A D SD   5. Good teachers are content knowledgeable but may need additional assistance with pedagogical strategies and techniques, and I feel comfortable about providing such assistance.

SA A D SD   6. I am familiar with pedagogical strategies and continually search for best practices to share with my teachers.

SA A D SD   7. Good teachers know much about the developmental needs of their students.

SA A D SD   8. Principals are familiar with learning styles and multiple intelligences theories and can help teachers apply them to instructional practice.

SA A D SD   9. I do not fully recognize the value of understanding teachers' skills and knowledge as a basis for their professional development.

SA A D SD   10. Goal setting is critical to teacher success in planning and preparing, and the principal should offer to collaborate with teachers in this area.

SA A D SD   11. I am familiar with curricular and teaching resources to assist teachers.

SA A D SD   12. I know I can help teachers develop appropriate learning activities suitable for students.

SA A D SD   13. I can help teachers plan for a variety of meaningful learning activities matched to school/state instructional goals.

SA A D SD   14. I would encourage teachers to use varied instructional grouping.

SA A D SD   15. I can assist teachers in developing a systematic plan for the assessment of student learning.

SA A D SD   16. I can provide professional development for teachers in planning and preparation.

The Classroom Environment

SA A D SD   1. I realize the importance of classroom management and discipline.

SA A D SD   2. I expect teacher interactions with students to be generally friendly and demonstrate warmth and caring.

SA A D SD   3. I expect teachers to develop a system of discipline without my assistance.

SA A D SD   4. I will play an active role in monitoring grade/school discipline plans.

SA A D SD   5. I support the classroom teachers in matters of discipline.

SA A D SD   6. I always communicate high expectations to all my teachers that they are the critical element in the classroom.

SA A D SD   7. I expect teachers to have a well-established and well-defined system of rules and procedures.

SA A D SD   8. I expect that teachers are alert to student behavior at all times.

SA A D SD   9. I can provide professional development to teachers in classroom management.

SA A D SD   10. As a teacher, I was a competent classroom manager.

Instruction

SA A D SD 1. I expect that teachers' directions to students are clear and not confusing.

SA A D SD 2. My directives to teachers about instruction are clear.

SA A D SD 3. My spoken language as a teacher was clear and appropriate according to the grade level of my students.

SA A D SD 4. I believe that teacher questioning techniques are among the most critical skills needed to promote pupil learning, and I feel comfortable in helping teachers frame good questions.

SA A D SD 5. Teacher questions must be uniformly of high quality.

SA A D SD 6. From my experience, teachers mostly lecture (talk) to students without enough student participation.

SA A D SD 7. I encourage teachers to encourage students to participate and prefer for students to take an active role in learning.

SA A D SD 8. I can provide a workshop for teachers on giving assignments that are appropriate to students, and that engage students mentally.

SA A D SD 9. I don't know how to group students appropriately for instruction.

SA A D SD 10. I am very familiar with grouping strategies to promote instruction.

SA A D SD 11. I can advise teachers on how best to select appropriate and effective instructional materials and resources.

SA A D SD 12. My demo lessons to teachers are highly coherent and my pacing is consistent and appropriate.

SA A D SD 13. I rarely provide appropriate feedback to my teachers.

SA A D SD   14. Feedback to my teachers is consistent, appropriate, and of high quality.

SA A D SD   15. I expect my teachers to rely heavily on the teacher's manual for instruction.

SA A D SD   16. I consistently encourage teachers to seek my advice on teaching and learning matters.

SA A D SD   17. I encourage teachers to use wait time effectively.

SA A D SD   18. I feel competent enough to give a workshop to teachers on effective use of wait time.

SA A D SD   19. I consider myself an instructional leader.

SA A D SD   20. Teachers perceive me as an instructional leader.

Professional Responsibilities

SA A D SD   1. I have difficulty assessing the effectiveness of teachers.

SA A D SD   2. I can accurately assess how well I am doing as an instructional leader.

SA A D SD   3. I really don't know how to improve teaching skills.

SA A D SD   4. I am aware of what I need to do in order to become an effective instructional leader.

SA A D SD   5. I rarely encourage parents to become involved in instructional matters.

SA A D SD   6. I actively and consistently engage parents to visit classrooms.

SA A D SD   7. I feel comfortable giving workshops to parents on curricular and/or instructional matters.

SA A D SD   8. I have difficulty relating to my colleagues in a cordial and professional manner.

SA A D SD   9. I collaborate with my colleagues in a cordial and professional manner.

SA A D SD   10. I avoid becoming involved in school projects.

SA A D SD   11. I rarely encourage teachers to seek to engage in professional development activities.

SA A D SD   12. I seek out opportunities for professional development to enhance my pedagogical skills.

SA A D SD   13. I am rarely alert to teachers' instructional needs.

SA A D SD   14. I serve teachers.

SA A D SD   15. I am an advocate for students' rights.

SA A D SD   16. I am an advocate for teachers' rights.

SA A D SD   17. I rarely encourage teachers to serve on a school-based committee.

SA A D SD   18. I enjoy working with teachers collaboratively on instructional matters.

Analyzing Your Responses

Note that the items above draw from research that highlights good educational practice. Review your responses and circle those that concern you. For instance, if you circled "Strongly Agree" for "I am rarely alert to teachers' instructional needs," ask yourself the following questions: "Why is this a problem?" "How can I remedy the situation?" "What additional resources or assistance might I need?" If you agree, share and compare responses with another educator. The dialogue that will ensue will serve as a helpful vehicle to move toward more effective practice.

In summary, review your responses for each of the four domains as noted here:

Domain 1—Planning and Preparation: This domain demonstrates your comfort level in working with teachers on content and pedagogical knowledge, knowledge of students and resources, ability to select instructional goals, and the degree to which you help them assess learning.

SA A D SD   1. My ability to work with teachers on planning and preparation is satisfactory.

Domain 2—The Classroom Environment: This domain assesses the degree to which you encourage and create an environment of respect and caring and establish a culture for learning related to many aspects of the classroom environment.

SA A D SD   1. I am satisfied that my ability to work with teachers in the classroom environment is satisfactory.

Domain 3—Instruction: This domain assesses the ability to work with teachers to communicate with clarity, use questioning and discussion techniques, engage students in learning, provide feedback to students, and demonstrate flexibility and responsiveness to student's instructional needs.

SA A D SD   1. I am satisfied that my knowledge and skills of instruction are satisfactory.

Domain 4—Professional Responsibilities: This domain assesses the degree to which you encourage teachers to reflect on teaching, maintain accurate records, communicate with parents, contribute to the school, grow and develop professionally, and show professionalism.

SA A D SD   1. I am satisfied I am professionally responsible.

Appendix F
Teacher Self-Assessment Questionnaire

Charlotte Danielson, in *Enhancing Professional Practice: A Framework for Teaching* (2007) published by the Association for Supervision and Curriculum Development, developed a framework or model for understanding teaching based on current research in the field. She identified "components" clustered into four domains of teaching responsibility: planning and preparation, classroom environment, instruction, and professional responsibilities. I developed the questionnaire below based on her framework. Please take the questionnaire because it will serve as an important reflective tool. A short activity to assess your responses can be found at the end of the questionnaire.

SA = Strongly Agree ("For the most part, yes")
A = Agree ("Yes, but . . . ")
D = Disagree ("No, but . . . ")
SD = Strongly Disagree ("For the most part, no")

Planning and Preparation

SA A D SD   1. I make many errors when I teach in my content area.

SA A D SD   2. I display solid content knowledge and can make connections with the parts of my discipline or with other disciplines.

SA A D SD   3. I rarely consider the importance of prerequisite knowledge when introducing new topics.

SA A D SD   4. Although I am content-knowledgeable, I need additional assistance with pedagogical strategies and techniques.

SA A D SD   5. I know the typical developmental characteristics of the age groups I teach.

SA A D SD   6. I have a solid understanding of learning styles and multiple intelligences theories and can apply them to instructional practice.

SA A D SD   7. I do not fully recognize the value of understanding students' skills and knowledge as a basis for my teaching.

SA A D SD   8. I don't believe that setting goals for my class is ever helpful because they may influence my expectations for them in a potentially negative way.

SA A D SD   9. I am very aware of teaching resources and seek to use them in preparing for lessons.

SA A D SD   10. I plan for a variety of meaningful learning activities matched to my instructional goals.

SA A D SD   11. I teach the whole class most of the time without utilizing instructional groups.

SA A D SD   12. My lessons are well-planned, organized, and matched to my instructional goals, most of the time.

SA A D SD   13. I have a well-defined understanding of how I will assess my students after a unit of instruction.

The Classroom Environment

SA A D SD   1. I realize I sometimes use poor interaction skills with my students, such as the use of sarcastic or disparaging remarks.

SA A D SD   2. My interactions with students are generally friendly and demonstrate warmth and caring.

SA A D SD   3. Students in my class, generally, don't get along with each other and conflicts are not uncommon.

SA A D SD   4. I convey a negative attitude toward the content suggesting that the content is mandated by others.

SA A D SD   5. I convey a genuine enthusiasm for the subject.

SA A D SD   6. Students in my class demonstrate little or no pride in their work and don't perform to the best of their ability.

SA A D SD   7. Students meet or exceed my expectations for high-quality work.

SA A D SD   8. I communicate high expectations for all my students.

SA A D SD   9. Students in my class are sometimes on-task, but often off-task behavior is observed.

SA A D SD   10. Transitions in my class occur smoothly, with little loss of instructional time.

SA A D SD   11. Routines for handling materials and supplies in my class are not well organized causing a loss of instructional time.

SA A D SD   12. I pride myself on the well-established system of rules and procedures in my class.

SA A D SD   13. I have difficulty enforcing standards for acceptable conduct in my class.

SA A D SD   14. I monitor student behavior and I am aware of what students are doing.

SA A D SD   15. I am alert to student behavior at all times.

SA A D SD   16. My classroom is safe, and the furniture arrangements are a resource for learning.

Instruction

SA A D SD   1. My directions are not clear to students, often causing confusion.

SA A D SD   2. My spoken language is often inaudible and crude.

SA A D SD   3. My use of questions needs improvement.

SA A D SD 4. I mostly lecture (talk) to my students without enough student participation.

SA A D SD 5. Only a few students participate in class discussions.

SA A D SD 6. My ability to communicate content is sound and appropriate.

SA A D SD 7. Activities and assignments are inappropriate for students and don't engage students mentally.

SA A D SD 8. I am very familiar with grouping strategies to promote instruction.

SA A D SD 9. I select inappropriate and ineffective instructional materials and resources.

SA A D SD 10. My lessons have little or no structure, and my pacing of the lesson is too slow, rushed, or both.

SA A D SD 11. I rarely provide appropriate feedback to my students.

SA A D SD 12. Feedback is consistently provided in a timely manner.

SA A D SD 13. I rarely, if ever, rely on the teacher's manual because I can adjust a lesson appropriate to the needs and level of my students.

SA A D SD 14. I often ignore students' questions or interests.

SA A D SD 15. I often blame my students for their inability to learn by attributing their lack of success to their background or lack of interest or motivation.

SA A D SD 16. I don't give up on slow learners and try to encourage them all the time.

SA A D SD 17. I tend to go off on tangents.

SA A D SD 18. I ask multiple questions that sometimes confuse students.

SA A D SD 19. I use wait time effectively.

Professional Responsibilities

SA A D SD   1. I have difficulty assessing my effectiveness as a teacher.

SA A D SD   2. I am aware of what I need to do to become an effective teacher.

SA A D SD   3. I don't have a system for maintaining information on student completion of assignments.

SA A D SD   4. I don't have a system for maintaining information on student progress in learning.

SA A D SD   5. I rarely encourage parental involvement in my class.

SA A D SD   6. I reach out to parents consistently.

SA A D SD   7. I collaborate with my colleagues cordially and professionally.

SA A D SD   8. I often volunteer to participate in school events.

SA A D SD   9. I generally avoid becoming involved in school projects.

SA A D SD   10. I rarely seek to engage in professional development activities.

SA A D SD   11. I am active in serving students.

SA A D SD   12. I am not an advocate for students' rights.

SA A D SD   13. I rarely desire to serve on a school-based committee.

Analyzing Your Responses

Note that the items above draw from research that highlights good educational practice. Review your responses and circle those that concern you. For instance, if you circled "Strongly Agree" for "I ask multiple questions that sometimes confuse students," ask yourself the following questions: "Why is this a problem?" "How can I remedy the situation?" "What additional resources or assistance might I need?" If you agree, share and compare responses with another educator. The dialogue will serve as a helpful vehicle to move toward more effective teaching practice.

In summary, review your responses for each of the four domains as noted below:

Domain 1—Planning and Preparation: This domain demonstrates your content and pedagogical knowledge, knowledge of students and resources, ability to select instructional goals, and the degree to which you assess student learning.

SA   A   D   SD   1. I am satisfied that my planning and preparation knowledge and skills are satisfactory.

Domain 2—The Classroom Environment: This domain assesses the degree to which you create an environment of respect and caring, establish a culture for learning, manage classroom procedures, manage student behavior, and organize physical space.

SA   A   D   SD   1. I am satisfied that my knowledge and skills of classroom environment are satisfactory.

Domain 3—Instruction: This domain assesses the ability to communicate with clarity, use questioning and discussion techniques, engage students in learning, provide feedback to students, demonstrate flexibility and responsiveness to student's instructional needs.

SA   A   D   SD   1. I am satisfied that my knowledge and skills of instruction are satisfactory.

Domain 4—Professional Responsibilities: This domain assesses the degree to which you reflect on teaching, maintain accurate records, communicate with parents, contribute to the school, grow and develop professionally, and show professionalism.

SA   A   D   SD   1. I am satisfied I am professionally responsible.

Appendix G
Supervisor's Perceptions about Teacher's Views Questionnaire

This survey assesses your attitudes and views about teachers' attitudes toward various aspects of the school's instructional program. In other words, how would teachers in your school respond to each item?

For each statement, indicate the extent to which you agree or disagree with the statement by circling the appropriate number.

Strongly Agree   = 5
Agree   = 4
Uncertain   = 3
Disagree   = 2
Strongly Disagree = 1

	SA	A	U	D	SD
1. Teachers willingly spend time before or after school to work on curriculum or other special school projects.	5	4	3	2	1
2. There is a feeling of togetherness in this school.	5	4	3	2	1
3. The principal provides instructional support to faculty regularly.	5	4	3	2	1
4. Decision-making in this school can be described as democratic.	5	4	3	2	1
5. Faculty are consulted about the school's goals or mission.	5	4	3	2	1
6. Teachers are treated as professionals.	5	4	3	2	1
7. Teachers feel threatened by supervisors.	5	4	3	2	1
8. There is a pessimistic atmosphere in this school.	5	4	3	2	1

9. Teachers feel lines of communication between the principal and teachers are open.	5 4 3 2 1
10. Faculty opinions are solicited but seldom used.	5 4 3 2 1
11. There is no opportunity for faculty growth to develop professionally.	5 4 3 2 1
12. Teachers enjoy working in this school.	5 4 3 2 1
13. The principal is accessible.	5 4 3 2 1
14. Teachers are free to share problems with the administration.	5 4 3 2 1
15. Parents actively support this school.	5 4 3 2 1
16. Teacher evaluation is used to threaten teachers.	5 4 3 2 1
17. There is a focus on student learning in this school.	5 4 3 2 1
18. Opportunities for staff development provided by my school meet my needs for professional growth.	5 4 3 2 1
19. Curriculum materials are readily available.	5 4 3 2 1
20. This is a well-managed school.	5 4 3 2 1
21. There is a clear and rigorous yet differentiated academic focus in this school.	5 4 3 2 1
22. The principal supports new teachers on an ongoing basis.	5 4 3 2 1
23. Professional development is ongoing, collaborative, and useful.	5 4 3 2 1
24. Teacher evaluation in this school is not very useful for me as a classroom teacher.	5 4 3 2 1
25. The school does not have clear goals and objectives.	5 4 3 2 1
26. Morale is high in this school.	5 4 3 2 1
27. Supervisory conferences are meaningful and helpful.	5 4 3 2 1
28. I am provided concrete feedback about my teaching on an ongoing basis.	5 4 3 2 1
29. This school is a learning community in that all or most teachers meet to discuss common problems.	5 4 3 2 1
30. The board is supportive of the school's instructional program.	5 4 3 2 1
31. There is an opportunity to meet with my supervisor about my teaching practice.	5 4 3 2 1
32. I have a professional growth plan.	5 4 3 2 1
33. Ample instructional materials exist to support my teaching.	5 4 3 2 1
34. New teachers are supported to manage their personal and professional time appropriately.	5 4 3 2 1

35. Release time is provided for professional development and additional training.	5 4 3 2 1	
36. I have a voice in the kind and type of professional development we have in this school.	5 4 3 2 1	
37. Principals frequently visit my classroom to offer instructional assistance.	5 4 3 2 1	
38. I receive adequate resources to support instruction.	5 4 3 2 1	
39. I usually meet with my supervisor after I am observed.	5 4 3 2 1	
40. I have an opportunity on occasion to visit my colleagues as they teach.	5 4 3 2 1	
41. My colleagues and I usually discuss student-related problems and issues as part of the regular school day.	5 4 3 2 1	
42. There is a genuine concern for teachers and students in this school.	5 4 3 2 1	
43. There is obvious conflict among administrative and supervisory personnel.	5 4 3 2 1	
44. I am supported by the administration in terms of student behavior.	5 4 3 2 1	
45. I am often given feedback on what I need to improve as a teacher.	5 4 3 2 1	
46. The curriculum in this school is written, discussed, understood, and revised every few years.	5 4 3 2 1	
47. All students have access to all curricula.	5 4 3 2 1	
48. Parents are partners in instruction and are encouraged to participate in this school.	5 4 3 2 1	
49. We meet as a grade to review student performance data.	5 4 3 2 1	
50. Our supervisor discusses the latest research in the field of teaching and education.	5 4 3 2 1	
51. The curriculum is mapped and well organized.	5 4 3 2 1	
52. Teachers have high expectations for student achievement.	5 4 3 2 1	
53. We are provided with the latest research on assessment.	5 4 3 2 1	
54. Judaic studies and general studies teachers meet on occasion to discuss common problems.	5 4 3 2 1	
55. There is no homework policy in this school.	5 4 3 2 1	
56. The supervisor does not effectively conduct classroom observations.	5 4 3 2 1	

57. The principal creates a supportive learning environment in this school.	5 4 3 2 1
58. The principal does not demonstrate leadership skills in the area of instruction.	5 4 3 2 1
59. The principal is more of a manager than an instructional leader.	5 4 3 2 1
60. Judging teacher competence is a fair process in this school.	5 4 3 2 1

Appendix H
Teacher Attitude Questionnaire

This survey assesses your attitudes and views about working in your school.

For each statement, indicate the extent to which you agree or disagree. As a reflective tool, after the questionnaire is administered, compare results with the preceding survey.

Strongly agree = 5
Agree = 4
Uncertain = 3
Disagree = 2
Strongly disagree = 1

	SA	A	U	D	SD
1. Teachers willingly spend time before or after school to work on curriculum or other special school projects.	5	4	3	2	1
2. There is a feeling of togetherness in this school.	5	4	3	2	1
3. The principal provides instructional support to faculty regularly.	5	4	3	2	1
4. Decision-making in the school can be described as democratic.	5	4	3	2	1
5. Faculty are consulted about the school's goals or mission.	5	4	3	2	1
6. Teachers are treated as professionals.	5	4	3	2	1
7. Teachers feel threatened by supervisors.	5	4	3	2	1
8. There is a pessimistic atmosphere in this school.	5	4	3	2	1
9. Teachers feel lines of communication between the principal and teachers are open.	5	4	3	2	1

10. Faculty opinions are solicited but seldom used.	5	4	3	2	1
11. There is no opportunity for faculty growth to develop professionally.	5	4	3	2	1
12. Teachers enjoy working in this school.	5	4	3	2	1
13. The principal is accessible.	5	4	3	2	1
14. Teachers are free to share problems with the administration.	5	4	3	2	1
15. Parents actively support this school.	5	4	3	2	1
16. Teacher evaluation is used to threaten teachers.	5	4	3	2	1
17. There is a focus on student learning in this school.	5	4	3	2	1
18. Opportunities for staff development provided by my school meet my needs for professional growth.	5	4	3	2	1
19. Curriculum materials are readily available.	5	4	3	2	1
20. This is a well-managed school.	5	4	3	2	1
21. There is a clear and rigorous yet differentiated academic focus in this school.	5	4	3	2	1
22. The principal supports new teachers on an ongoing basis.	5	4	3	2	1
23. Professional development is ongoing, collaborative, and useful.	5	4	3	2	1
24. Teacher evaluation in this school is not very useful for me as a classroom teacher.	5	4	3	2	1
25. The school does not have clear goals and objectives.	5	4	3	2	1
26. Morale is high in this school.	5	4	3	2	1
27. Supervisory conferences are meaningful and helpful.	5	4	3	2	1
28. I am provided concrete feedback about my teaching on an ongoing basis.	5	4	3	2	1
29. This school is a learning community in that all or most teachers meet to discuss common problems.	5	4	3	2	1
30. The Board is supportive of the school's instructional program.	5	4	3	2	1
31. There is an opportunity to meet with my supervisor about my teaching practice.	5	4	3	2	1
32. I have a professional growth plan.	5	4	3	2	1
33. Ample instructional materials exist to support my teaching.	5	4	3	2	1
34. New teachers are supported to manage their personal and professional time appropriately.	5	4	3	2	1

35.	Release time is provided for professional development and additional training.	5	4	3	2	1
36.	I have a voice in the kind and type of professional development we have in this school.	5	4	3	2	1
37.	Principals frequently visit my classroom to offer instructional assistance.	5	4	3	2	1
38.	I receive adequate resources to support instruction.	5	4	3	2	1
39.	I usually meet with my supervisor after I am observed.	5	4	3	2	1
40.	I have an opportunity on occasion to visit my colleagues as they teach.	5	4	3	2	1
41.	My colleagues and I usually discuss student-related problems and issues as part of the regular school day.	5	4	3	2	1
42.	There is a genuine concern for teachers and students in this school.	5	4	3	2	1
43.	There is obvious conflict among administrative and supervisory personnel.	5	4	3	2	1
44.	I am supported by the administration in terms of student behavior.	5	4	3	2	1
45.	I am often given feedback on what I need to improve as a teacher.	5	4	3	2	1
46.	The curriculum in this school is written, discussed, understood, and revised every few years.	5	4	3	2	1
47.	All students have access to all curricula.	5	4	3	2	1
48.	Parents are partners in instruction and are encouraged to participate in this school.	5	4	3	2	1
49.	We meet as a grade to review student performance data.	5	4	3	2	1
50.	Our supervisor discusses the latest research in the field of teaching and education.	5	4	3	2	1
51.	The curriculum is mapped and well organized.	5	4	3	2	1
52.	Teachers have high expectations for student achievement.	5	4	3	2	1
53.	We are provided with the latest research on assessment.	5	4	3	2	1
54.	Judaic studies and general studies teachers meet on occasion to discuss common problems.	5	4	3	2	1
55.	There is no homework policy in this school.	5	4	3	2	1
56.	The supervisor does not effectively conduct classroom observations.	5	4	3	2	1

57.	The principal creates a supportive learning environment in this school.	5	4	3	2	1
58.	The principal does not demonstrate leadership skills in the area of instruction.	5	4	3	2	1
59.	The principal is more of a manager than an instructional leader.	5	4	3	2	1
60.	Judging teacher competence is a fair process in this school.	5	4	3	2	1

Appendix I
Best Annotated Works and Resources for Promoting Instructional Excellence

The literature on the subject at hand and related areas are extensive. This list is not meant to serve as a comprehensive resource by any means. The selected titles I have annotated are few but, in my opinion, are among the most useful references on the subject regardless of the date of publication. I encourage individuals or teams of school leaders to read selected books and periodicals as a means of personal/team professional development. The titles listed here below are my current favorites but feel free to select your own.

Caveat: Don't remain complacent now that you have, perhaps, completed a master's or even a doctoral degree. Keep up your professional development. Spend one hour a week exploring websites, and text resources, including articles from magazines, journals, and books related to teaching, curriculum, professional development, supervision, and evaluation. As a leader, you influence by example.

Vignette: Katia Rodriguez, a middle school principal, shares with her faculty books and other resources that she uses. Then, she asks teachers at a faculty meeting to select a book from an annotated list she composed. She asks volunteers to form groups of four to select a book that each member of the group will read. She will order the book for each member of the group, and the group will have a month to read it. Then, at the next monthly faculty meeting, she allows teachers, in groups, to discuss their common book. Dr. Rodriguez shares some possible questions for the group to discuss such as, "What idea(s) can we put into practice in our classroom tomorrow morning?" At the next faculty meeting, each group reports to the whole faculty and shares information about the book and the manner in which they will try to implement a lesson or two. In following meetings, faculty report on the success or even lack thereof of their attempt to implement ideas for practice. All the groups share and learn from each other.

INSTRUCTIONAL LEADERSHIP CLASSICS

Blase, J., & Blase, J. (2004). *Handbook of instructional leadership: How successful principals promote teaching and learning.* Corwin. https://us.corwin.com/en-us/nam/handbook-of-instructional-leadership/book226257

This is a classic volume and one of the most comprehensive treatments of instructional leadership that provides fascinating insights into actions and strategies leaders should take to promote instructional quality. The new edition expands the scope of the topic by explicating in concrete ways how instructional leaders inspire their staff to develop professional learning communities. This book is both a theoretical exposition and a practical guide to maximizing teaching and learning.

Fullan, M. (2008). *What's worth fighting for in the principalship?* Teachers College Press. https://michaelfullan.ca/books/whats-worth-fighting-principalship/

Michael Fullan is a world-renowned expert on school change. Arguably, this is his classic work on the subject, although he has published many books. There are practical guidelines for implementation. Fullan masterfully interweaves extant research with practical strategies. This volume is a short and quick read. Be sure to explore more of his works.

Glickman, C. D., & West Burns, R. (2020). *Leadership for learning: How to bring out the best in every teacher.* Association for Supervision and Curriculum Development. https://www.ascd.org/books/leadership-for-learning-how-to-bring-out-the-best-in-every-teacher-2nd-edition?variant=121007

This book is practical guidance to help teachers improve classroom teaching and learning. Instructional supervisors can read this volume with teachers as a conversation piece. The book is easy to use and is reader friendly.

Shaked, H. (2022). *New explorations for instructional leaders: How principals can promote teaching and learning effectively.* Rowman & Littlefield. https://rowman.com/ISBN/9781475868753/New-Explorations-for-Instructional-Leaders-How-Principals-Can-Promote-Teaching-and-Learning-Effectively

Professor Haim Shaked is the premier researcher in the field of instructional leadership today. You must visit his webpage https://haimshaked.com/. This work is a masterpiece and a must-read reference work. He asks and answers key questions: Why do principals find it difficult to put instructional leadership into action? What can help them overcome the challenges involved in applying instructional leadership? What functions of instructional leadership do school leaders tend to sidestep?

Whitaker, T. (2020). *What great principals do differently: 20 things that matter most.* Taylor & Francis. https://www.routledge.com/Study-Guide-What-Great-Principals-Do-Differently-Twenty-Things-That-Matter/Whitaker-Whitaker-Zoul/p/book/9780367550028

Ultimately, regardless of strategies, it's the principal who makes the most difference in promoting excellence. This book is a classic that will offer much food for thought.

Zepeda, S. J. (2012). *The principal as instructional leader: A handbook for supervisors.* Eye on Education-Routledge. https://www.routledge.com/The-Principal-as-Instructional-Leader-A-Practical-Handbook/Zepeda/p/book/9781596672215

A very helpful and useful workbook accompanied by a CD that contains electronic versions of many forms provided throughout. Explore other works by Professor Zepeda since she is among the major leaders in school leadership in the world.

BEST BOOK ON TEACHING

Wong, H. K., & Wong, R. T. (1998). *How to be an effective teacher: The first days of school.* Harry K. Wong Publications. http://www.harrywong.com/

Of course, there are many important teaching books (see below). But this is the one I'd recommend first. It's been a national best-seller year after year. Wong is an inspirational speaker, and his book is a must-read not only for every beginning teacher, but also for experienced teachers who might need to be reminded of the basics and need some inspiration.

OTHER BOOKS RECOMMENDED FOR TEACHERS

Canter, L. (1992). *Assertive discipline.* Lee Canter and Associates. https://www.eln.co.uk/blog/assertive-discipline-approach-of

-behaviour-management#:~:text=Assertive%20discipline%20is%20a%20systematic,being%20able%20to%20control%20it and https://helpfulprofessor.com/assertive-discipline/

    This is the very best book on corrective discipline. Learn and practice the three "response styles." Although controversial (some hate the system, others swear by it), I'm in the latter camp. Recommend it! A lifesaver!! See excellent YouTube videos for techniques in action.

Ducker, B., & Holmberg, C. (2023). *Feedback for continuous improvement in the classroom: New perspectives, practices, and possibilities.* Sage.

    This book is a very useful and practical guide to implementing effective feedback to students, which is a critical and necessary element of good teaching.

Ginott, H. G. (1993). *Between teacher and child.* Macmillan. https://www.goodreads.com/en/book/show/822263

    If I could recommend only one book on nurturing the relationship between a teacher and a student, this is it! Sensitive, insightful, and practical, this work is a classic in the field.

Hattie, J. (2008). *Visible learning.* Routledge. https://visible-learning.org/

    John Hattie's groundbreaking research sheds light on teaching strategies that influence positive student learning. Teachers can learn much from the results of his research. Although criticized by some, his work stands as significant as it helps teachers and supervisors promote student learning.

Lemov, D. (2010). *Teach like a champion: 49 techniques that put students on the path to college.* Jossey-Bass. https://malaysia.kinokuniya.com/bw/9780470550472

    Although not traditionally research-based, this book is filled with practical teaching techniques that have relevance to classroom instruction. Some of the strategies appear rigid and manipulative, but it's well worth a read. It's a great work to share with faculty during faculty or department meetings. See the excellent YouTube videos for many of the techniques in action.

INSTRUCTIONAL STRATEGIES

Gregory, G. H., & Chapman, C. (2012). *Differentiated instructional strategies: One size doesn't fit all.* Corwin.

    I am a big believer in differentiation. This book, already a classic, offers practical strategies and techniques.

Harmin, M. (2006). *Inspiring active learning: A complete handbook for today's teachers.* Association for Supervision and Curriculum

Development. https://www.ascd.org/books/inspiring-active-learning?variant=103113E4

If I could only recommend one book for you to read on practical strategies to promote learning, then this book would be it! It's a bit dated, but relevant as ever.

Orlich, D. C., Harder, R. J., Callahan, R. C., Treysan, M. S., & Brown, A. (2012). *Teaching strategies: A guide to effective instruction.* Cengage Learning. https://www.amazon.com/Teaching-Strategies-Guide-Effective-Instruction/dp/1111832633

In its 10th edition, this book is very practical with many strategies and techniques clearly explained.

Tomlinson, C. A. (2004). *How to differentiate instruction in mixed-ability classrooms.* Association for Supervision and Curriculum Development. https://www.amazon.com/Differentiate-Instruction-Mixed-Ability-Classrooms/dp/013119500X

Carol Ann Tomlinson, an influential educator, provides easy-to-read and useful practical strategies for how teachers can navigate a diverse classroom. If you want to learn how to teach students of different abilities at the same time, read this book. Included are great case studies of classrooms at all levels in which instruction is differentiated successfully. This book is a classic.

BEST BOOKS ON CURRICULUM

Ullah, O. (2020). *Role of principals in curriculum development and implementation.* Scholars Press. https://www.amazon.com/Role-Principals-Curriculum-development-Implementation/dp/6138936639#:~:text=The%20role%20of%20a%20principal,discipline%2C%20and%20implementation%20of%20curriculum

There aren't, unfortunately, many books on curriculum development for school leaders. This lamentable fact is due, in large measure, to the proliferation of prepackaged curricula and state-national curricular standards imposed by fiat. This book, however, is a very good exposition of the principal's role in supporting teaching and learning through curriculum development.

Wiggins, G., & McTighe, J. (2011). *The Understanding by Design (UbD) guide to creating high-quality units.* Association for Supervision and Curriculum Development.

UbD is the best, most practical, and most effective curriculum design in my opinion. There are many books on UbD. They are all good and practical.

BEST BOOK ON TEACHER PROFESSIONAL DEVELOPMENT

Dunn, R., & Hattie, J. (2021). *Developing teaching expertise: A guide to adaptive professional learning design.* Sage. https://us.sagepub.com/en-us/nam/developing-teaching-expertise/book267564

This book presents a commonsense approach to designing professional development for teachers on understanding "what works best" for classroom teachers. Parenthetically, I want to reemphasize a point I made earlier in this book that too much of the research-based literature doesn't provide practical guidelines for classroom teachers. My book, *Creating a Culture of Excellence: A School Leader's Guide to Best Practices in Teaching, Curriculum, Professional Development, Supervision, & Evaluation* is meant to translate research into practical strategies. I fondly recall reading a book in college by John Holt in which he decried the lack of interest among researchers to provide classroom assistance with practical, research-based strategies. See, Holt, J. C. (1970). *What do I do Monday?* Dutton. https://www.goodreads.com/en/book/show/573004

Hattie, J. (2012). *Visible learning for teachers: Maximizing impact on learning.* Routledge. https://visible-learning.org/

This book is a valuable resource that can be used in professional development for teachers to provide concrete and practical teaching strategies. Not about professional development per se, but given its focus and content, is among the most useful resources.

BEST BOOKS ON SUPERVISION

Glickman, C. D., Gordon, S. P., Ross-Gordon, J. M., & Solis, R. D. (2023). *SuperVision and instructional leadership: A developmental approach.* Pearson.

In its 11th edition, this work is the best-selling book on the subject. Carl Glickman is a pioneer in the field of supervision. Steve Gordon is a prolific and distinguished author in the field. The book presents a good balance between the theory and research of supervision with practical suggestions for implementation.

Sullivan, S., & Glanz, J. (2013). *Supervision that improves teaching: Strategies and techniques.* Corwin. https://www.amazon.com/Supervision-That-Improves-Teaching-Learning/dp/1452255466

More of a workbook filled with practical tools for teacher observation, techniques for differentiating supervision, and alternative approaches to traditional supervision, this popular book, in its 4th edition, emphasizes empowering teachers to reflect on their teaching in an ongoing, nonjudgmental manner.

BEST BOOKS ON EVALUATION

Darling-Hammond, L. (2013). *Getting teacher evaluation right: What really matters for effectiveness and improvement.* Teachers College Press. https://www.amazon.com/Getting-Teacher-Evaluation-Right-Effectiveness/dp/0807754463
: There aren't many good practical works on the subject, but famed researcher Linda Darling-Hammond has written a book that presents a comprehensive teacher evaluation system based on research and best practices. Personally, I haven't seen many evaluation systems in practice that really help teachers improve. To my mind, evaluation is a tool to assess a teacher's basic competence. Hence, it only serves as an accountability and not an improvement function. To work with teachers on improving teaching, supervision is better suited for that essential purpose. The next author (see below) disagrees with me.

Marshall, K. (2013). *Rethinking teacher supervision and evaluation.* Jossey-Bass. https://www.marshallmemo.com/articles/Rethinking.pdf
: This updated version is an excellent resource on supervision and evaluation. Although I personally may not agree with his entire approach, Kim Marshall (author of *The Marshall Memo*, https://marshallmemo.com/. A MUST SUBSCRIPTION FOR EVERY EDUCATOR) provides several excellent ways for school leaders to effectively improve their school's instructional program. The book raises the question of why we need a new approach to supervision and evaluation in the first place. Then it methodically outlines a new approach that is clearly presented and practical. This book will be appreciated by practitioners.

Stronge, J. H. (2005). *Evaluating teaching: A guide to current thinking and best practice.* Corwin. https://www.amazon.com/Evaluating-Teaching-Current-Thinking-Practice/dp/1412909783
: The author is a highly respected educational researcher, and he has written a useful guide to designing and implementing a teacher evaluation program. In the book, a "Teacher Self-Evaluation Tool Kit" is discussed that is a valuable resource. Within this book, see: Airasian, P., & Gullickson, A. (2006). Teacher self-evaluation (pp. 186–211).

Appendix I

RESEARCH ON INSTRUCTION AND TEACHING

Explore these major research publications in the field:
- *The Handbook of Research on Teaching*—https://www.jstor.org/stable/j.ctt1s474hg
- *International Handbook on Teacher Quality*—https://www.routledge.com/International-Handbook-of-Teacher-Quality-and-Policy/Akiba-LeTendre/p/book/9781138890787
- *Review of Educational Research*—https://journals.sagepub.com/home/rer
- *Review of Education*—https://bera-journals.onlinelibrary.wiley.com/journal/20496613
- *Teaching and Teacher Education*—https://www.sciencedirect.com/journal/teaching-and-teacher-education
- *International Society for Technology in Education (ISTE)*—https://www.iste.org/

Danielson, C. (2007). *Enhancing professional practice: A framework for teaching.* Association for Supervision and Curriculum Development. https://www.ascd.org/books/enhancing-professional-practice-a-framework-for-teaching-2nd-edition?variant=106034

   This noted international author has developed a popular framework or model for understanding teaching based on extant research in the field.

Marzano, R. J., Pickering, D. J., & Pollock, J. E. (2012). *Classroom instruction that works: Research-based strategies for increasing student achievement.* Association for Supervision and Curriculum Development. https://www.amazon.com/Classroom-Instruction-That-Works-Research-Based/dp/0871205041

   The authors examine decades of research in education to come up with nine teaching strategies that have positive effects on student learning. This is a must-read.

Porter, A. C., & Brophy, J. (1988). Synthesis of research on good teaching: Insights from the work of the Institute for Research on Teaching. https://files.ascd.org/staticfiles/ascd/pdf/journals/ed_lead/el_198805_porter.pdf

   A bit dated, but this article is a classic and much, if not all, of the practical information in it is as relevant today as it was when it was first published.

Rosenshine, B. (2012). Principles of instruction: Research-based strategies that all teachers should know. *American Educator, 12,* 12–19, 39–40.

One of the most respected educational researchers who made a significant impact in helping teachers teach with excellence. This work is also a must-read.

Stronge, J. H. (2018). *Qualities of effective teachers*. Association for Supervision and Curriculum Development. https://www.amazon.com/Qualities-Effective-Teachers-James-Stronge/dp/1416625860

This volume is one of the best summaries of research on teacher effectiveness.

RESEARCH ON SCHOOL REFORM AND IMPROVEMENT

Barr, R. D., & Yates, D. L. (2010). *Turning your school around: A self-guided audit for school improvement.* Solution Tree. https://www.solutiontree.com/free-resources/schoolimprovement/tysa

Learn a step-by-step protocol for the self-guided audit that focuses on the most critical areas of school improvement. The authors give readers a realistic view of the work involved in a top-to-bottom audit while providing supporting researched-based evidence of its effectiveness.

Jakubowski, C. (2022). Leading for school change in a divided community. *Journal of Educational Supervision, 5*(2). https://doi.org/10.31045/jes.5.2.5

This case study focuses future administrators on the real-life conflicts inherent in supervision and employee rights. The case study examines the inherent power dynamics in trying to affect change.

Zepeda, S. J., Lanoue, P. D., Rivera, G. M., & Shafer, D. R. (2022). *Leading school culture through teacher voice and agency.* Routledge. https://www.taylorfrancis.com/books/mono/10.4324/9781003222651/leading-school-culture-teacher-voice-agency-sally-zepeda-philip-lanoue-grant-rivera-david-shafer

This work, led by an influential and well-respected professor of education, is a comprehensive, practical treatise on reshaping school culture through collaborative work among key constituents.

SELECTED SCHOLARLY RESEARCH PUBLICATIONS

Please note that many excellent peer-reviewed scholarly articles have been published in each of the five areas noted here. These are simply my personal favorites.

Teaching

Campbell, R. J., Kyriakides, L., Muijs, R. D., & Robinson, W. (2010). Differential teacher effectiveness: Towards a model for research and teacher appraisal. *Oxford Review of Education, 29*(3), 347–362. https://www.tandfonline.com/doi/abs/10.1080/03054980307440

This article reviews the research on teacher effectiveness and provides an excellent overview of the history of the subject. It argues for an approach to examining teaching effectiveness that is nuanced and differential dependent on context and other factors.

Shulman, L. S. (1986). Those who understand: Knowledge growth in teaching. *Educational Researcher, 15*(2), 4–31.

Professor Lee Shulman is the elder statesman in the education field whose contributions to the study of teaching are as widely acknowledged as they are groundbreaking.

Shulman, L. S. (1987). Knowledge and teaching: Foundations of the new reform. *Harvard Educational Review, 57*(1), 1–22. http://hepg.org/her-home/issues/harvard-educational-review-volume-57,-issue-1/herarticle/foundations-of-the-new-reform_461

His research on pedagogical content knowledge and pedagogy, in general, have been formative and influential.

Curriculum

There are many scholarly articles published in prominent peer-reviewed journals. Please peruse https://resources.nu.edu/c.php?g=630945&p=4408617.

Professional Development

Balta, N., Amendum, S. J., & Fukkink, R. G. (2023). The effect of job-embedded professional development on teacher and student outcomes: A multi-level meta-analysis. *International Educational Review*. https://int-er.com/download/the-effect-of-job-embedded-professional-development-on-teacher-and-student-outcomes-a-multi-level-12961.pdf

Job-embedded professional development refers to teacher learning that is grounded in day-to-day teaching practice and is designed to enhance teachers' content-specific instructional practices with the intent of improving student learning. This article is a good study on the subject.

Supervision

Gordon, S. P. (2019). Educational supervision: Reflections on its past, present, and future. *Journal of Educational Supervision*, (2). htttps://doi.org/https://doi.org/10.31045/jes.2.2.3

A preeminent scholar of supervision, Professor Gordon summarizes the vast supervision literature along with personal reflections and recommendations for understanding supervision's past, present, and future.

Evaluation

Berliner, D. (2018). Between Scylla and Charybdis: Reflections on and problems associated with the evaluation of teachers in an era of metrification. *Education Policy Analysis Archives*, 26(54), 1–24. https://doi.org/10.14507/epaa.26.3820

A critical and brilliant analysis by an influential preeminent educational researcher.

Hallinger, P., Heck, R., & Murphy, J. (2014). Teacher evaluation and school improvement: An analysis of the evidence. *Educational Assessment, Evaluation, and Accountability*, 26(1), 5–28._https://doi.org/10.1007/s11092-013-9179-5

Three of the most prestigious researchers in the field present a cogent analysis of extant research on the impact of evaluation on school improvement.

Hazi, H. M. (2022). Reconsidering the dual purposes of teacher evaluation. *Teachers and Teaching*, 28(7), 811–825. https://doi.org/10.1080/13540602.2022.2103533

Perhaps the most renowned researcher and commentator on teacher evaluation, Professor Helen Hazi acknowledges that evaluation, as practiced internationally, tends to focus on the delivery of feedback, rather than on improving teaching. Yet she argues persuasively that it's time to rethink teacher evaluation and place its emphasis on supporting teacher learning.

Popham, W. J. (2013). On serving two masters: Formative and summative teacher evaluation. *Principal Leadership*, 13(7), 18–22. http://www.nassp.org/Content/158/PLmar13_popham.pdf

Professor James Popham is widely acknowledged as the field's expert on assessment.

Other notable researchers and authors that readers should explore who made a significant impact on instruction are Gloria Ladson Billings, James Burnett, David Coleman, John Dewey, Adriana Di Prato, Rita Dunn, Richard

Elmore, Jose Ferreira, Paulo Freire, Howard Gardner, Thomas L. Good. John Goodlad, Philip Hallinger, Clara Hemphill, Salman Kahn, David Kolb, Kenneth Leithwood, Megan Tschannen-Moran, Jeannie Oakes, Alan C. Ornstein, William E. Pinar, Ray C. Rist, Kenneth Robinson, Patrick Slattery, and Ralph Tyler. I apologize if I missed anyone.

Moreover, there are many international individuals, for instance, whom I have not included because I am simply unaware of them. That is my shortcoming. I am situated within my culturally bound purview.

I would, however, like to state that we have been blessed by brilliant educators all over the world who aim to improve learning on a daily basis. Although the outstanding individuals mentioned in this appendix are certainly noteworthy since they have published their work, I would like to acknowledge, and forgive me for using an oft-used expression, the "unsung heroes," who are classroom teachers from preschool through graduate school who work with children and adults daily to enhance their learning experiences.

WEBSITES

- www.corwinpress.com
  Popular book publisher: Peruse its website for the latest books/conferences, etc.
- www.ascd.org
  The Association of Supervision and Curriculum Development: Popular book publisher. Peruse its website for the latest books/conferences, etc.
- https://www.aera.net/
  The American Educational Research Association: A national research society that strives to advance knowledge about education, encourage scholarly inquiry related to education, and promote the use of research to improve education.
- http://www.nassp.org/
  National Association of Secondary School Principals
- http://www.naesp.org/
  National Association of Elementary School Principals
- https://blog.feedspot.com/educational_leadership_blogs/
  Leadership blogs
- https://www.infoagepub.com/vc/NAPDS23
  An amazing array of books and resources to promote instructional quality.
- https://www.topeducationdegrees.org/lists/5-great-websites-for-school-administrators/
  Five great websites for school administrators.

Appendix I

- https://www.teachersoftomorrow.org/blog/insights/teacher-websites/
  Sites for teachers.
- https://www.cis-spain.com/en/best-educational-leadership-magazines/
  Best educational leadership magazines.
- https://library.csp.edu/educational_leadership/leadership
  List of scholarly peer-reviewed journals in educational leadership.
- https://guides.libraries.uc.edu/teachingactivites/talp
  Best teaching resources.
- https://www.education.vic.gov.au/Documents/school/teachers/support/high-impact-teaching-strategies.pdf
  Evidence-based teaching practices.
- https://www.prodigygame.com/main-en/blog/teaching-strategies/
  Practical teaching strategies.
- https://www.techlearning.com/resources/top-sites-for-educator-professional-development
  Best professional development for teachers.
- https://www.educationcorner.com/teaching-blogs/
  Best blogs on teaching.
- https://www.wallacefoundation.org/knowledge-center/Documents/The-School-Principal-as-Leader-Guiding-Schools-to-Better-Teaching-and-Learning.pdf
  A useful resource on instructional leadership.
- https://www.edweek.org/leadership/what-works-and-what-doesnt-in-teacher-pd/2022/10
  What works in PD (*Education Week*, 2022).
- https://www.techlearning.com/resources/top-sites-for-educator-professional-development
  Tech learning.
- https://www.edutopia.org/school-leadership-principals-teachers-resources
  Professional development for school leaders.
- https://educationwalkthrough.com/11-resources-to-help-you-become-an-effective-evaluator/
  Interesting resources that support teacher evaluation.
- https://www.prodigygame.com/main-en/blog/teacher-evaluation/
  Good blog on evaluation.
- https://learningforward.org/2019/05/30/what-makes-curriculum-work-4-lessons-for-administrators/
  Good information on curriculum development.
- https://files.ascd.org/staticfiles/ascd/pdf/siteASCD/publications/UbD_WhitePaper0312.pdf
  Good resource for using Understanding by Design.

- https://blog.eduplanet21.com/3-stages-of-the-understanding-by-design-template-eduplanet21
  Good blog on curriculum development.
- https://digitalcommons.usf.edu/jpr/
  The *Journal of Practitioner Research* is an open-access journal that contains peer reviewed articles that are especially relevant for teacher and school administrator practitioners.
- https://digitalcommons.library.umaine.edu/jes/
  The *Journal of Educational Supervision* publishes peer reviewed articles related to the field of supervisory practices in education. It is the premier journal in the field that educational leaders will find invaluable.

Finally, the Rowman & Littlefield School Leadership Series: Bridging Theory and Practice
- https://rowman.com/Action/SERIES/_/RLBTP/Bridging-Theory-and-Practice

There are several good leadership series available from different publishing houses, but this series aims to bridge theory with practice, which is its advantage. Published books always include practical recommendations for implementation. Information regarding the following books can be accessed via the link above:

Brown, K. M. (2008). *Preparing future leaders for social justice, equity, and excellence: Bridging theory with practice through transformative androgogy.* Rowman & Littlefield.

Brown, K., & Shaked, H. (2018). *Preparing future leaders for social justice: Bridging theory and practice through a transformative andragogy* (2nd ed.). Rowman & Littlefield.

Glanz, J. (Ed.). (2021). *Crisis and pandemic leadership: Implications for meeting the needs of students, teachers, and parents.* Rowman & Littlefield.

Glanz, J. (Ed.). (2021). *Managing today's schools: New skills for school leaders in the 21st century.* Rowman & Littlefield.

Lavigne, A. L., & Derrington, M. L. (Eds.). (2023). *Actionable feedback for PK–12 teachers.* Rowman & Littlefield.

Locke, L. A., & Hayes, S. D. (2024). *Bridging leadership and school improvement.* Rowman & Littlefield.

Rabinowitz, C., & Reichel, M. (2023). *Principal recruitment and retention: Best practices for meeting the challenges today.* Rowman & Littlefield.

Shaked, H. (2022). *New explorations for instructional leaders: How principals can promote teaching and learning effectively.* Rowman & Littlefield.

Snyder, K. J., & Snyder, K. M. (Eds.). (2023). *Systems thinking for sustainable schooling: A mindshift for educators to lead and achieve quality schools.* Rowman & Littlefield.

Snyder, K. M., & Snyder, K. J. (Eds.). (2024). *Regenerating education as a living system: Success stories of systems thinking in action.* Rowman & Littlefield.

Stader, D. (2012). *Leadership for a culture of school safety: Linking theory to practice.* Rowman & Littlefield.

Zepeda, S. J. (Ed.). (2018). *Making learning job-embedded: Cases from the field of educational leadership.* Rowman & Littlefield.

Zepeda, S. J. (Ed.). (2018). *The job-embedded nature of coaching: Lessons and insights for school leaders.* Rowman & Littlefield.

Zepeda, S. J. (Ed.). (2008). *Real world supervision: Adapting theory to practice.* Rowman & Littlefield.

Appendix J
Sample Instructional Audit Report

SUMMARY OF STRENGTHS

Teachers

- Teaching at XYZ is of high quality. Teachers engaged students, by and large, in active learning, checked for understanding, and care very much about each student's educational progress. We were particularly impressed with several of the recent hires who appear to be outstanding educators. Although a formal program with adequate professional development for teacher mentoring doesn't exist, new teachers receive adequate mentoring from their supervisors and, in some cases, from fellow teachers. Teachers in the school feel supported. Teachers discuss teaching practices on an ongoing basis in formal and informal ways. [Evidence: Observations of classrooms form the basis of this conclusion as well as interviews with teachers.]

Staff

- Dedicated faculty who care about furthering the academic and social development of the students is evident. Teachers are passionately committed to XYZ's mission. [Evidence: Interviews and interactions with teachers, most of whom without prompting, pointed out their commitment to their "care" for students. Administrators too highlighted their concern for students. XYZ is a student-centered school.]

Early Childhood Center

- Warm, nurturing early childhood learning and experiences are provided utilizing appropriate philosophies and pedagogies. The facilities and materials are superior. XYZ should be proud of its early childhood program and continue to herald it in the wider community. [Evidence: Interviews and interactions with early childhood educators and classroom observations support this finding and experience in assessing similar programs in North America. The program is NAEYC accredited, which is indicative of the program's excellence.]

iPads in the Middle School

- Although there were problems with program implementation, we observed the appropriate use of iPads to guide and facilitate top-quality instruction. Students, in the classrooms, used the devices as instructional tools to enhance learning. Teachers, it seemed, felt comfortable with their use and seamlessly incorporated them to enhance the learning experiences in the classroom. [Evidence: Observations in classrooms and interviews with teachers and students.]

School Discipline and Classroom Management

- Students are well behaved, and it is obvious that the administrators and teachers have created a safe and nurturing learning environment for students. Although there is no school-wide discipline plan (there are of course guidelines offered), each teacher has their own approach that appears to be quite effective. Classrooms display classroom rules for behavior in an effective and clear manner. For instance, one classroom posted the following:
Don't Strike Out
1st Strike: First warning
2nd Strike: Talk at recess/lunch
3rd Strike: Write a strike letter to me in your free time
Beyond: Your parents must sign strike letter.

There is a clear and effective use of assertive discipline. [Evidence: Observations of classroom interactions and the manner in which teachers administer discipline formed the basis for this conclusion.]

The Physical Plant and Instructional Materials

- Although not directly related to the school's instructional program, the physical plant (inside and outside) is an asset and simply magnificent. The environment plays a key role in supporting quality instruction. Teachers, students, parents, and administrators must feel proud of its facilities that establish a conducive learning atmosphere. Classrooms and hallways are clean and beautifully decorated. Ample instructional materials are evident. Learning centers in classrooms are well-supplied and utilized appropriately.

SUMMARY OF FINDINGS REGARDING SCHOOL XYZ'S INSTRUCTIONAL PROGRAM

Opportunities for Growth

Introduction to Reviewing XYZ's Instructional Program

The purpose of this review is to provide school officials with suggestions in the area of educational/instructional services to enable them to determine the degree to which the school is meeting its educational objectives and to define opportunities to strengthen the educational program. We offer these recommendations based on our understanding of best practices in the field as well as working with many exemplary schools in North America. Administrators are encouraged to reflect upon issues and questions raised in this report. The hope is that the administrators will review the recommendations offered, and together with their assessment of the school's instructional program, develop an action plan over the course of the next three to five years to build upon its substantial successes and bring XYZ to an even higher level of educational performance.

Potential Opportunities for Enhancing XYZ's Instructional Program

The recommendations suggested below are made in light of our understanding of the unique characteristics that exist in this particular school. The goal is to suggest improvement focus areas that build on XYZ's successes and will support instructional improvement in an incremental, yet substantive manner. It should also be noted that we were impressed by the fact that all of the educators and board members we met with welcomed any suggestions we would make to improve instructional delivery and educational quality in the school.

The school community (internally) should be proud of its accomplishments. Instructionally, XYZ is a good school.

A word about prioritization of these areas is in order. Generally, school leadership will assess the viability of these areas/recommendations and then construct a strategic action plan for prioritization and implementation based on their better understanding of the school's resources, personnel, and otherwise.

Teaching—Questions to stimulate thinking about teaching practices: How do we know what effective teaching looks like? Do we have agreed-upon criteria for good teaching?
- Finding:
  - There does not appear to be a common vision of effective teaching. Although administrators created rubrics for use with teachers in classroom observations, teachers were not consulted in advance about the creation of these criteria.
- Recommendation:
  - Commence conversations about a common vision of good teaching, perhaps at faculty meetings. Provide opportunities for deep discussions, accept differences of opinion, gather extant research on effective teaching, and incorporate intervisitations (releasing teachers to observe each other and perhaps visiting other schools to observe teaching practices, etc.). This process should take about a year and in the end, a common rubric should emerge that the entire teaching community at XYZ accepts.

Professional Development—Questions to stimulate thinking about professional development (PD): What is the purpose of a PD program? Who should develop such a program and why? What are the criteria of good PD? What is the connection between PD and teacher behavior in the classroom? What is its effect on student achievement?
- Findings:
  - Although XYZ has provided professional development opportunities for teachers, it has been inconsistently employed and not developed strategically.
- Recommendation:

    Develop a PD program—Much of professional or staff development in many schools is content-weak, episodic, and at its worst, irrelevant to the needs of teachers. As instructional leaders, principals realize that well-conceived, planned, and assessed PD is vital to improving teaching and student learning. Best practice in PD points to several components

as necessary. We encourage XYZ faculty and administration to consider these criteria:
- *Purposeful and articulated*—Goals for a PD program must be developed, examined, critiqued, and assessed for relevance. These goals must be stated in some formal way so that all educators concerned with the PD program are clear about its intent and purpose. Has XYZ collaboratively (with teachers assuming leadership) developed purposeful goals that are published in advance of the start of the new year?
- *Participatory and collaborative*—Too often PD is top-driven, even at times by administrative fiat. Such programs are less effective because teachers, for whom PD serves the greatest benefit, are not actively involved in its design, implementation, and assessment. Best practice in PD requires wide participation by all stakeholders. Some teachers noted that they are rarely consulted regarding PD.
- *Knowledge-based and discipline-based*—PD must be based on the most relevant and current research in the field. Also, teachers will not value PD unless it contains, in the words of one teacher, "some substance, . . . something I can take back to the classroom." Also, one size shouldn't fit all. For instance, ESL teachers may need special PD that may differ from that of subject specialty teachers.
- *Focused on student learning*—According to one advocate of best practice in PD, "Educators must never forget that the objective of PD is to increase student learning." Principals and committees that are responsible for planning PD programs should consider first and foremost the teacher behaviors or activities that most directly impact student learning and then "work backward to pinpoint the knowledge, skills, and attitudes educators must have."
- *Ongoing*—Too much professional development is of the one-shot variety. A leader delivers a workshop, for instance, then leaves without any follow-up. Such efforts have marginal value at best. PD opportunities must be made on a continuous basis so that ideas and practices are sustained. PD cannot impact classroom practice in a significant way unless workshops and programs are continually offered with sustained follow-up.
- *Developmental*—PD must not only be ongoing but developmental, that is, building gradually on teacher knowledge and skills in a given area or topic.
- *Analytical and reflective*—PD opportunities must promote instructional dialogue and thinking about teaching practice and purposefully address ways of helping students achieve more. Also, PD must be continuously assessed in terms of its relevance and value to teachers.

160   *Appendix J*

   Although XYZ addresses some of these criteria for PD, it should meet all of them as enumerated above. Teachers reported that too many topics are covered with insufficient depth. Administrators and teachers, during a faculty meeting, can decide on an area or theme they'd like to pursue, say over the course of a school year, or even two. It should be noted that XYZ does utilize some of its teachers in sharing PD with colleagues. This is good practice and should be encouraged to a greater extent.

How to accomplish this recommendation:

- Select a focus for PD at a given school level. For instance, the Lower School might want to focus on formative assessment.
- Start small—Select one subject or grade to start.
- Form a committee of volunteers—Put together a group of one administrator and two or three teachers to develop a sequence of PD initiatives to educate faculty in formative assessments—a year-long plan of PD should be offered. PD initiatives should be sequentially developed with follow-ups in teacher classrooms with consultants offering assistance as needed. Aligning with a college or university, for instance, would be a low- or no-cost way of obtaining presenters for such workshops.
- Conduct workshops—use videotapes, visit schools that have implemented initiatives, etc.
- Establish modest goals, solicit volunteers among the faculty to lead the way, and establish assessment criteria for PD in this area.

Evaluation and Supervision—Questions to stimulate thinking about supervision are: What are some ways we might differentiate our approach to supervision among different cohorts of teachers? Do all teachers need annual evaluations? How might we develop strategies to continue the professional growth of teachers?

- Findings:
  - Supervision of instruction does occur at XYZ. Supervisory practices, however, are quite traditional and lack the incorporation of cutting-edge strategies. Supervision via walk-thru, etc. is inspectional in nature and does not lend itself to professional growth. A greater variety of supervisory approaches are needed.
- Recommendations:
  A. The school's supervision program should offer a variety of supervisory strategies, briefly outlined below (please note that none of these

strategies should be implemented without fully preparing teachers about their purpose and benefits):

a. Clinical Supervisory Model—With the assistance, perhaps, of a consultant, the administration should start to incorporate a clinical supervision (preconference, short observations, and a postconference) process that encourages deep reflection about teaching practices. With this model, supervisors do not "tell" teachers what is "right" or "wrong" (as is evident on XYZ teacher evaluation forms) but rather offer data (through the use of observation forms or instruments) and then begin an instructional conversation with the teachers encouraging them to reflect on their practices in the classroom.
b. Demo Lessons and Videotaping/Intervisitations—Faculty meetings should include, at times, analyses of videotaped teaching episodes (perhaps a supervisor can first volunteer to have themself videotaped for 10 minutes, to then be used for viewing and discussion by a group of teachers). Such practices build trust and a learning community in the school. Discuss teaching and instruction on an ongoing basis. Avoid meetings that do not actively involve faculty in learning how to improve their teaching. Cost implications: none, other than building meeting times into schedules, even contractually.
c. Intervisitations—Many teachers we interviewed reported that they rarely have seen a colleague teach. Providing release time for colleagues to observe each other and then provide time for discussion is recommended. We know this occurs in some instances. We are suggesting, however, that the process be more formalized. Colleagues who observe each other can later share their experiences at a department or whole faculty meeting. All meetings should be instructional in nature (not merely administrative, for example, making announcements that could be done via memo or email). Use of that time for collaboratively developed PD by department or subject is recommended.
d. Peer coaching—Teachers alternate periods observing each other and use data to engage in conversations. Peer coaching may differ from the strategy above in the sense that such observations are long term.
e. Action research—Encouraging teachers, in lieu of the traditional observation requirement (this is useful for tenured, experienced teachers), to engage in a project in which they identify (on their own or with a colleague) a problem they are experiencing in the classroom, compose some research questions, gather data to

answer them, reflect on findings, take actions, etc. is an invaluable supervisory asset.

f. Book studies—Distribute copies of a book (on pedagogy, or in a particular discipline) and then engage in meetings, in conversations about strategies learned for classroom implementation. Have participants report on their work to the larger faculty at one of the scheduled faculty or departmental meetings.

g. Reflective journaling—Again, an alternative to traditional supervision might be to offer teachers choices to record journal reflections of their teaching over time to be then shared, in discussion, with another colleague or presented at a faculty meeting, etc.

h. Lesson studies—Teachers collaboratively plan a lesson (perhaps in association with the curriculum mapping process), each presents the lesson to a class, and then meet together to discuss successes, questions, and challenges. See, for example, Stepanek et al., *Leading lesson study: A practical guide for teachers and facilitators* (2007).

i. Instructional rounds—A small group of teachers and others visit the classroom of a colleague. There are various models used for such rounds (see, e.g., http://www.marzanoresearch.com/documents/Marzano_Protocol.pdf).

***More Effective Integration and Employment of Teaching Assistants*—**
Questions to stimulate thinking about the use of assistants are: What is the purpose of assigning an assistant to a particular classroom? Are the roles of assistants clearly defined and known by all participants? How can assistants be most effectively utilized to aid instruction/differentiation?

- Findings:
  - Assistants we interviewed reported that they perform mundane, low-level functions such as office copying, dealing with paperwork, bulletin board construction, etc. Also, coordination between assistants and teachers needs improvement. Assistants need PD in terms of how best to work with selected students.
- Recommendations:
  - Assistants should be utilized to tutor individuals or work with small groups of students much more than they are currently.
  - "Ongoing" PD must be offered to prepare assistants to most effectively aid instruction in the classroom. Additionally, teachers need PD on how best to utilize assistants (when and how).

Tracking and Inclusion—Questions to stimulate thinking about the use of tracking classes are: What is the purpose of tracking? What impact may it have on children's social and emotional learning? Are there alternatives to tracking? How can XYZ promote more inclusionary practices?

- Finding:
  - Tracking is commonly employed in both lower- and especially middle schools. Students have internalized labels used by the school: "Oh, I'm in the advanced class." "I'm 7b." "I'm in LEAP." Tracking students, educators explain, allows "us to teach to the appropriate level of the students thus meeting their educational needs." The extent to which teachers are attuned to the educational, emotional, and social needs of students with disabilities varies greatly. In our discussions with some staff, it appears that tracking may have an emotional toll on some students at XYZ. Other teachers we spoke with were unaware of the possible negative effects of extensive tracking. Still, attention to the needs of students with disabilities and the tracking issue is required.
- Recommendations:

An Alternative to Tracking—Tracking is useful and does serve an educational purpose. However, overuse or inappropriate use of tracking can negatively affect students' emotional and academic progress. We would encourage the school to examine more inclusive practices and pedagogies that are discussed in educational literature.

We do not recommend detracking for all classes at once. Rather, we are suggesting that the school examine the feasibility of detracking classes in, say, one subject/grade at first, after, of course, extensive PD by the teacher in differentiated instruction and inclusive practices.

[Included in this section is a brief literature review on the benefits of inclusionary practices, not included in this appendix.]

We suggest the school examine the feasibility of detracking some classes but with sufficient and appropriate PD for teachers to learn how best to meet the needs of all ability levels within the same classroom.

Other Observations

The points that follow are not major areas of concern at this time, nor do they necessarily impact AYZ's overall instructional program, but we do encourage the school to consider them:

1. Is there an alternative way to report student progress without quantifying learning ability artificially? We've seen other elementary and middle schools utilize more descriptive assessments of student progress (we can provide examples from other schools). Consider portfolios or anecdotals to replace the current progress report cards that utilize academic level numbers. Also, grade keys are nebulous. Comments made on report cards are sometimes sketchy ("Student A could work harder") and too general (e.g., Student B's reading has improved"). Consider more descriptive accounts (e.g., "Student A submitted her mid-term project by providing only two artifacts to support her position. She could have conducted further research by . . . " or "Student B's decoding skills and word recognitions have improved to the extent to which she is able to . . . "). Ensure sufficient time for teachers to complete such anecdotals.
2. Are there ways to further strengthen teacher knowledge of current research and practice in the field? We didn't see a teacher resource center that included the latest journals, publications, instructional videos, and DVDs. We recommend that the school subscribe to ASCDs *Educational Leadership* magazine and *The Marshall Memo*.
3. Might we recommend that teachers record on the board during each lesson an aim, objective, or what many schools now call a "teaching point"? Doing so will focus students' efforts and assist with planning and assessment.
4. Improved articulation could occur during transitions from nursery school to kindergarten, Grades 4 to 5, 6 to 7, and 8 to high school. In other words, what are the expectations of middle school teachers for student writing? Have middle school teachers met with lower school teachers to discuss writing expectations?
5. Although the hallways are decorated with beautiful pictures, designs, and prefabricated materials, we suggest that the bulk of displays be of students' work.
6. We heard a few educators use the terms "regular education" and "special education." We'd recommend the avoidance of the term "regular ed" in favor of "general ed." By implication "nonregular ed" (i.e., special education) classes might subtly be perceived as "irregular."
7. Consider the pros and cons of having students read aloud in class, which may lead to some students feeling embarrassed; the way in which teachers call on students (watch the use of wait time and more distribution among all students); the lack of formal library instruction for upper graders; and overuse of frontal teaching in math, science, and social studies.

Appendix K
The Instructional Goals Matrix

Target Area	Teaching	Curriculum Enhancement	Professional Development	Supervision	Evaluation
Specific Goal(s)					
Assessment Tool(s)					
The Plan—Steps Involved					
Desired Outcome Relating to Instruction					
Person(s) Responsible for Oversight					
Time Frame					
Associated Costs					

Index

bridging theory with practice, xi, 25, 152, 167, 169–70

change: knowledge, 3, 78; suggestions for, 45–46, 52, 70–71, 157; teacher behavior, 24, 35–36, 64, 159
curriculum: best book, 142; development, 11, 13–14, 32, 54–71, 143, 146–47, 157; false assumptions, 14; models (UbD/Tyler's Rationale), 55, 57–58, 144; pre-packaged, 11, 13, 61, 110, 143; process, 61; quality, 54–71, 101; research-based practices, 63; state-imposed, 14, 143; tripod view, 30, 55–56

Danielson, Charlotte, 12, 33, 117, 125, 146
Darling-Hammond, Linda, ix, xii, 27, 29, 56, 145
David, Jane, 76
Dewey, John, 51, 149, 167
Dunn, Rita, 144, 149

education, approaches to, viii, 32–33, 67, 72, 76, 145
evaluation: best book, 145; false assumptions, 18; self-evaluation, 72, 145; teacher (problems), 17–18, 71–74, 76, 80, 145, 149, 160, 165; versus supervision, 33, 160

Fullan, Michael, 3–4, 19, 24, 78–81, 90, 140

Glickman, Carl, x, xii, 23, 67, 140, 144

Hallinger, Philip, vii, xii, 2, 149–50
Hattie, John, 9, 19, 142, 144
Hazi, Helen, ix, xii, 18, 71–72, 149, 170
Holt, John, 144

instruction: approaches to, 32–33, 67, 72, 78, 145; inclusion, viii; principles of, 51, 75, 146; process, viii, 3, 9, 35–36, 56, 66, 115
instructional leadership: assumptions of, 25, 28; concept of, ix; emergence of, 2–3; field of, vii, ix; core, 4, 23; effective, 4; practices of, x, 24, 46; references on, xii, 116, 140–41, 144
instructional quality: audits, 5, 9, 31, 147, 155; promoting excellence, 141; reports on, 11–12

leadership: forms of, 25, 115; series, xi, 152, 167, 169–70; transformational, 3–4, 78–81 learning activities, 9, 10, 13, 14, 15, 17, 18, 26, 28, 30, 33, 34, 37, 49, 52, 53, 57–58, 62, 65, 70, 73, 83, 89

Marshall, Kim, 43, 85, 145, 164

Nadelstern, Eric, 28
notes, 21, 43, 76, 91

Popham, James, 50, 71, 149
principal and schools: as an effective leader, 2, 61; as instructional leader, ix–x, 2–5, 25–27
professional development (PD): best practices, 62–65, 158–60; false assumptions, 15; research-based practices, 55
professional learning community: ix, 4, 30, 79, 80, 83

questionnaires, ix–x, 5, 93, 97, 103, 113, 117, 125, 131, 135

Rosenshine, Barak, 51, 146

Sarason, Seymour, 78
schools: as communities, 10, 170; instructional quality, viii, 1, 5, 9–12, 13, 14, 16, 17, 23, 30–31, 45, 69, 76, 91; site visits, 6–8; as moral institutions, 72, 81
Sergiovanni, Thomas, 2, 24
Shaked, Haim, 2, 5, 24, 40, 75–76, 140, 152
Shulman, Lee, 148
student achievement, 4, 24–25, 27, 47, 53, 64–65, 81
supervision: action research, 29, 67, 82, 84–91; best books, 144–45; book studies, 67, 82, 84, 87, 88, 162; demos, 67, 69; dog-pony show, 16; false assumptions, 17; growth plans, 68; intervisitations, 11, 67, 158, 161; lesson studies, 68, 80, 84, 88, 162; PCOWBIRDS, 66, 68; peer coaching, 67, 87, 91, 161; as professional development, 15, 62–65, 158–60; research-based practices, 47; walk-throughs, 16, 76, 82, 84

teacher evaluation: false assumption, 13, 14, 15, 17, 18; formative and summative, 58, 59, 149; practical guidelines, 142; and school improvement, 33, 76; self-evaluation, 72, 145
teaching: academic engaged time, 47–48; academic instructional time, 47–48; academic success time, 47–48; active learning, 12, 19, 47, 50–53, 76, 84, 142, 155; allocated time, 47; best book, 141–42; checking for understanding, 9, 32, 46, 47, 48, 50, 81; definition, 9–10; differentiation, 11, 35, 53, 142, 162; false assumptions, 13; frontal, 10–12, 21, 31–32, 83–86, 164; minute paper, 12, 34, 50; pair-share, 49, 50, 83; persistence of recitation, ix, 1, 10, 110; reciprocal, 21, 35, 50, 75, 83; research-based practices, 66–69; tripod view, 30, 55, 56; wait time, 16, 32, 47, 49, 70, 80, 164
Tomlinson, Carol Ann, 12, 143
Tyler, Ralph, 55, 57, 58, 150

vignettes, 13, 14, 15, 16, 18, 25, 28, 29, 31, 34, 36, 37, 53, 62, 65, 66, 139

Wiggins, Grant, 58, 143

Zepeda, Sally, 16, 141, 147

About the Author

Jeffrey Glanz is a professor and head of the MEd program in leadership and management in educational systems at Michlalah Jerusalem College, Israel. He held the Silverstein Endowed Chair in Professional Ethics and Values and was a tenured professor of education and administration at the Azrieli Graduate School of Yeshiva University, New York. He was dean of graduate studies and chair of education at Wagner College in Staten Island, New York. He was executive assistant to the president at Kean University (New Jersey) and at Kean was named Graduate Teacher of the Year by the Student Graduate Association. He was also the recipient of the Presidential Award for Outstanding Scholarship. He was a teacher and school administrator in the New York City public schools for 20 years.

Professor Glanz has authored, coauthored, edited, and coedited 26 books on various educational topics, including six books with Rowman & Littlefield Publishers: *Revisiting Dewey: Best Practices for Educating the Whole Child Today* (2010, coauthored with Daniel Stuckart); *Action Research: An Educational Leader's Guide to School Improvement* (2014, author); *Supervision: New Perspectives in Theory and Practice* (2015, coedited with Sally Zepeda); *Crisis and Pandemic Leadership: Implications for Meeting the Needs of Students, Teachers, and Parents* (2021, editor); *Managing Today's Schools: New Skills for School Leaders in the 21st Century* (2022, editor); and this book, *Creating a Culture of Excellence: A School Leader's Guide to Best Practices in Teaching, Curriculum, Professional Development, Supervision, and Evaluation*.

Professor Glanz is also the series editor of the Rowman & Littlefield School Leadership Series: Bridging Theory and Practice, which aims to solicit educational leadership manuscripts. Consider submitting a book proposal.

Call for Submissions

The Rowman & Littlefield Leadership Series: Bridging Theory and Practice

Edited by Jeffrey Glanz, Michlalah-Jerusalem College, Israel

What are we seeking? This international series reflects the latest cutting-edge theories and practices in school leadership. Uniquely, we seek manuscripts that bridge the perennial divide between theory and practice. The Series motto is framed after Kurt Lewin's famous statement, and we paraphrase, that there is no sound theory without practice and no good practice that is not framed on some theory.

Authors will be expected to illustrate the intimate and integral connection between the two divides. For instance, a volume may address a new theory in educational or school leadership but implications for practice are expected. We purposely did not identify specific areas or topics we are interested in publishing because we are open to almost any proposal that combines practice and theory. A volume doesn't necessarily have to present implications for the international arena, although, if relevant, we certainly welcome such proposals. The audience will be practitioners, professors at the undergraduate and graduate levels, and policymakers.

What's in it for you? One of the invaluable lessons I, Jeffrey, learned from my dad, a Holocaust survivor, was that life is about growth, making your mark, and helping others in the process. As a contributing author to this Series imagine the contributions you could make to the field of educational leadership. Envision the audience you could reach. Think about the education practitioners and future educational leaders reading your book who will likely garner ideas for transforming the way children are educated, and how schools and school systems are or should be managed. If you have ideas that you want to share with current and future education leaders, then this is the Series for your book.

Therefore, anyone involved or interested in school leadership, from teacher leaders to leaders of teachers, to those who work with and teach them, is welcome to submit a proposal. Contact Jeffrey Glanz, the series editor, to obtain information and publishing guidelines for submitting a book proposal.

Proposals will be reviewed by the Series Editor and the Bridging Theory and Practice Advisory Board for relevancy, clarity, and ingenuity in the school leadership field. Distinguished scholars on the Bridging Theory and Practice Advisory Board include:

Köksal Banoğlu, National Ministry of Education, Istanbul, **Turkiye**
Clair T. Berube, Virginia Wesleyan University, Virginia, **USA**
Stephen P. Gordon, Texas State University, Texas, **USA**
Sedat Gumus, The Education University of Hong Kong, **Hong Kong, SAR**
Helen M. Hazi, West Virginia University at Morgantown, West Virginia, **USA**
Jessica Holloway, Australian Catholic University, Queensland, **Australia**
Shazia Rehman Khan, Bahria University, **Pakistan**
Benjamin Kutsyuruba, Queen's University–Kingston, ON, **Canada**
Fiona Longmuir, Monash University, **Australia**
Chanina Rabinowitz, The Hebrew University of Jerusalem, **Israel**
Susan Sullivan, The College of Staten Island, CUNY, **USA**
Melissa Tuytens, Ghent University, Ghent, **Belgium**

Submit proposals, questions, or concerns to Jeffrey Glanz at yosglanz@gmail.com (see www.jeffreyglanz.com). The series editor welcomes all queries from anyone interested in submitting a formal book proposal or discussing potential ideas.

www.ingramcontent.com/pod-product-compliance
Lightning Source LLC
Chambersburg PA
CBHW020122010526
44115CB00008B/937